Case Studies in Economic Development

Case Studies in Economic Development

Stephen C. Smith
The George Washington University

Longman
New York & London

Case Studies in Economic Development

Longman, 10 Bank Street, White Plains, N.Y. 10606

Associated Companies:
Longman Group Ltd., London
Longman Cheshire Pty., Melbourne
Longman Paul Pty., Auckland
Copp Clark Pitman, Toronto

Senior acquisitions editor: David M. Shapiro
Development editor: Susan Alkana
Production editor: Ann P. Kearns
Cover design: Betty L. Sokol
Production supervisor: Richard C. Bretan

Library of Congress Cataloging-in-Publication Data

Smith, Stephen C. Date.
Case studies in economic development / Stephen C. Smith
p. cm.
ISBN 0-8013-1289-2
1. Developing countries—Economic conditions—Case studies.
2. Economic development—Case studies. I. Title.
HC59.7.9553 1993
330.9172 4—dc20

93-15189
CIP

1 2 3 4 5 6 7 8 9 10-CRS-9796959493

TABLE OF CONTENTS

Introduction.

In ten years of teaching development economics I have found that students grasp general principles and models of development much better if they also are presented with case studies that clearly illustrate those principles. At the same time, where there is sharp controversy, students appreciate the debate much better if the contending approaches are presented in a context of case studies.

Economists participating in multidisciplinary courses, or teaching courses largely attended by noneconomics students (as I sometimes do), often need to be attentive to making connections to approaches of other disciplines; but wish to do so in a way that does not compromise the integrity of economics as a discipline.

Use of the right case studies can help accomplish these objectives.

Moreover, development economics is simply made much more interesting if very current development issues that students may be following in the news are integrated into the course. Students demand a real-world feel from their development courses, and better appreciate core theory material if they can see how it relates to that real world in more than just passing anecdotes. Unfortunately, no text has stressed case studies, though the new 5th Edition of Michael P. Todaro's Economic Development contains 18 country overviews, as well as four new comparative case studies prepared by me. Nevertheless, no conventional text can hope to stay current on development topics and countries in the news. These case studies have grown out of these goals and concerns.

Case Studies in Economic Development strives to represent alternative points of view on development in a balanced way. For one thing, this means that the centrality of market development is stressed without overlooking the role of government policy. The prevalence of market failure in development is examined without overlooking the recurring problems of government failure. Finally the text is one of mainstream economics at core but open to contributions of other disciplines and nonmainstream approaches in development economics when they may help guide wise implementation of policy. This in my experience is the best way to help students to understand the nature of development controversies.

This is a new kind of text and a new kind of publishing. The number of case studies will grow annually, and good contributions from development instructors are very welcome.

Here is a list of the studies that may be available for early 1994. Several of these were suggested by professors planning to use the book. The specific country applications are tentative. Feedback on which of these topics and countries would be of the greatest interest would be especially welcomed.

Likely new case studies:

Growth vs. Development: Brazil and Costa Rica
Different Theories of Development: Explaining the Case of Mexico Africa falls behind: debate over the causes
Development on a large scale: The Mahaveli project in Sri Lanka
Recent cross-national evidence on growth and the GNP of nations Growth and Inequality: Exploring the Connection
Fertility and Economic insecurity: Women in Rural Nigeria
Negative consequences of elitist education systems: Tanzania
How has a Debt-for-Nature Swap Worked in Practice?: Bolivia
Inside the Household: Java
Exchange rates really matter: cross-national evidence
Population and Development: India
Rostow's Stages of Growth: Brazil
Restrictive policy toward multinationals: Argentina and Korea
Yugoslavia: Lessons from the Causes of National Dissolution
Loss of fishing resources in the Philippines: causes and response Creating Financial Markets: Malaysia
International comparisons: real, nominal and purchasing power
Corruption: Nigeria
Case illustrating the Second Best
Sequencing of liberalization in a second best world: India
Balanced vs. unbalanced growth
The role of labor markets in LDCs
New growth theories--relevance for LDCs
The Poverty Trap
Financial Repression: India
The role of international organizations in development: World Bank
Surplus labor: China
Trade vs. aid: Does Foreign Aid Really Help?
Intellectual property rights: Taiwan
North--south models (product cycle)
Inflation (structuralist vs. monetarist)

Big Bang Strategies: Poland
An emerging common market: Argentina, Brazil, Uruguay, and Paraguay

The sequence of the studies is designed in part to follow the chapter order of Michael Todaro's Economic Development, Fifth Edition, 1993. Chapters 5 through 17, the topical chapters in Todaro's text, are closely matched by the topics in the case studies. The first four case studies introduce students to development problems and themes, though they do not precisely match the theory and overview sections of the text. The first two cases on Taiwan and Zaire introduce students to the huge range of development experiences and outcomes. In the forthcoming expanded and revised version of this book, among many other new case studies, at least two chapters will be added which more closely follow the early text themes. These are tentatively slated as Growth vs. Development: Brazil and Costa Rica; Different Theories of Development: Explaining the Case of Mexico.

Also in the next edition, I am likely to add simple diagrams and tables of data for most cases. Again, any comments on projected topics and suggestions of new ones, or recommendations on supplementary materials, will be appreciated.

I would like to thank David Shapiro and Susan Alkana at Longman Press for their supportive participation in the project, Michael Todaro for helpful suggestions, Ira Gang for valuable comments on the complete manuscript, Anindita Mukherjee for her suggestions on the sharecropping study, and Catherine Bealin for excellent research assistance.

1. Taiwan--Inside the Miracle: A Development Success Story

Taiwan is one of the four East Asian "tigers," or "mini-dragons," whose dramatic economic successes of recent decades, along with South Korea, Singapore and Hong Kong, have influenced the way economists think about development. With a population of about 21 million, Taiwan is a mountainous, 14,000-square-mile island off the coast of China, about the combined size of Massachusetts, Connecticut and Rhode Island.

Taiwan's claim to its status as a "development miracle" is as strong as that of any other economy in the world. The island has racked up a measured annual economic growth rate averaging close to 9% over more than four decades. Taiwan grew nearly 10% annually in the widely used benchmark 1965-80 period, higher than any other reported figure. Though growth in various countries has occasionally reached rates as high as 14%, and in some regions as high as 25% or more, Taiwan's average growth performance is the highest ever recorded over such a long stretch of time. In the postwar period, Taiwan has grown from an impoverished annual per capita income of just $100, to a relatively prosperous society with per capita income measured at close to $10,000 U.S. dollars. At least as important, Taiwan has achieved universal elementary and middle school education (9 years are mandatory), and a healthy population with a life expectancy of 71.9 years for men and 77.2 for women, and an infant mortality rate of only five per thousand. Absolute poverty has been essentially eliminated, there is very little unemployment, and there is and relative inequality is modest even by developed country standards.

Taiwan thus seems to have achieved almost everything we look for in development. This achievement is in dramatic contrast to many other economies that started in a similar--or even much better--set of circumstances in the postwar world. The question begs itself: how did they do it.

Explanations for Success. Paradoxically, but as is often the case in development studies, the problem is not that we have too few explanations for success or failure, but too many. Taiwan's success in particular has been ascribed to many factors. Here are 14 of the major ones: 1) emphasis on education; 2) extensive infrastructure development; 3) early and thorough land reform; 4) very high rates of savings and investment; 5) a mixture of constructive foreign influences and diffusion of commercial ideas from Japan and the United States; 6) effective government industrial planning; 7) the free market's release of human energies and creativity; 8) the 1960s Vietnam War boom; 9) direct American aid--and the fact that Taiwan used that aid for investment rather than consumption; 10) the work ethic and productive attitudes of the labor force; 11) a long history as an entrepreneurial culture; 12) the initiation of an export-led growth strategy in the midst of the rapidly expanding world economy of the early 1960s; 13) the movement into entrepreneurship of capable local islanders seeking opportunities for advancement, as they were blocked from the political arena; and 14) the survival instinct--the necessity of economic development as a defense against attack from the mainland (the Peoples' Republic of China).

We will be able to dismiss perhaps four of these explanations as major factors. But any of just a few of the remaining factors might offer sufficient explanation for Taiwan's success. The case of Taiwan's development may thus be "overdetermined." Despite advances in such techniques as cross-national econometrics, we still lack adequate ways of measuring factors of development across countries. Uncovering the key factors in any one "development miracle" thus remains almost as much art as science.

Emphasis on education. Consistent with the historical Chinese cultural veneration for education, six years of education became compulsory on Taiwan in 1950. This was remarkable enough--but more remarkable still in the troubled history of developing economies was the fact that this edict was actually carried out within just a few years. Especially impressive were enrollment rates for girls, which surpassed 90% for those aged 6-11 by 1956. (The comparable figure for boys in that year was over 96%.) Emphasis on girls' education is one of the most important factors in successful development--if not the single most vital factor, as the case study on girls' education in Pakistan demonstrates.

When compulsory education was expanded to a full nine years in 1968, there were doubts that the economy could afford it. Today, while nine years remains a remarkable minimum educational standard for any developing economy, plans are being considered to expand compulsory schooling to twelve years.

Some other features: Students go to school 7 hours per day, for five and one-half days per week. In 1992-93, the student-teacher ratio was just 26 for elementary school, 21 for junior high, and 22 each for academic and vocational high schools. Teacher salaries are relatively high, comparable to lower-middle management in Taiwan. The U.S. was Taiwan's model for general education and Japan for vocational education. Greater emphasis is placed on general rather than job-specific skills. But incentives for close relationships between education and business are also stressed. In one innovative program, vocational high school teachers are paid to work in industry during the summer months, to stimulate the development of curriculum relevant to industry's current needs. Tax breaks are given for company donations of personnel and equipment to schools.

Extensive infrastructure development. Development of infrastructure has been widely cited as a crucial factor in successful development by economists such as Paul Rosenstein-Rodan and Albert Hirschman. A major highway, for example, is argued to represent a "growth pole" around which industrial and commercial development can consolidate and grow. Post-War Taiwan inherited an infrastructure system from the period of Japanese colonial rule (1905-1945) that was far superior to that of most poor countries. The Japanese built roads, ports, and railroads to facilitate their own acquisition of rice and other farm products from the island. But this same infrastructure became a vehicle for national industrial growth from the 1950s. This endowment was supplemented by the government's own extensive program in the 1950s and 1960s. Taiwan's army was too large for the island, a legacy of the pre-1949 control of the mainland by the governing Kuomintang, or Chinese Nationalists. Thousands of soldiers participated in a voluntary program to retire from active military service to build infrastructure, including the technically challenging east-west highway projects--a program reckoned in Taiwan to be a major factor in its subsequent success.

Early and thorough land reform. Not being burdened by close political ties to landlords, the Taiwan government was politically able to implement a thoroughgoing land-to-the-tiller reform program in the 1950s. Land owners received stock in state owned enterprises in return for transferring land to peasants. This was a major factor in the extremely rapid growth of agricultural productivity in this period--a crucial foundation for later industrialization. Other countries with similar land reform efforts, such as South Korea and Japan, have seen impressive results. The U.S. analogously benefitted from nineteenth century programs such as the Homestead Act. Development in Latin American countries has been severely hampered by the lack of land reform.

Very high rates of savings and investment. Capital formation has long been deemed crucial to successful development. Developed countries have much higher levels of capital per head than less developed countries, one of the factors enabling developed countries to enjoy higher productivity and incomes. Taiwan's savings rates were among the highest ever recorded, reaching 30-40% in the 1950s and 60s.

The savings ethic is deeply rooted in Taiwanese culture. Parents teach children the overriding need to save for a rainy day. This cultural pattern is supplemented by public policies which keep real interest rates for savers relatively high and tax free. Interestingly, like fellow tiger South Korea but unlike Singapore, Taiwan has a relatively low foreign capital share in total investment, about 10%. High savings and investment is an important factor in development, but not a sufficient one. India has substantially increased its rates of investment since independence, but not its growth rate--in part because capital equipment is more expensive there, in part because investments have not been made in the most productive sectors at any point in time.

Diffusion of commercial ideas. High saving alone will not create a development miracle without productive ideas among entrepreneurs about what use to make of it. Though hard to document precisely, Taiwan has had considerable success at absorbing commercial ideas from Japan and the United States. Much of this was due to the diligence of thousands of individual small companies. But government also played a role, through agencies like the China External Trade Development Council (CETDC), which combed the world, especially the United States, for ideas on how Taiwan firms could upgrade and adapt to enter industrial markets. The World Bank's Donald Keesing has offered some fascinating insights into its operation:

"Market research in CETDC's New York office as of 1980 was based on an active search for items that could be sold in the United States. The search began with an analysis of the size and origin of US imports, followed by a preliminary study of the price and quality of the more competitive imported and US products. From this the officers in New York reached an estimate of the likelihood of Taiwan, China firms competing successfully against offerings already on the market. (They claimed to understand the manufacturing capabilities of Taiwan, China firms well enough to do this.) Once a likely product was identified, the office asked firms in Taiwan, China to send it samples of the product and price lists. Representatives of the office would then visit importers, wholesalers, and other traders with samples and price lists, prospecting for sales. They would try to get reactions to the product. If the buyers were interested they would telex the manufacturers. If not, they would find out why and then suggest appropriate steps to the manufacturer."

This leads us to perhaps the most complex set of development issues--the roles of state and market in successful development.

Effective government industrial planning. A traditional explanation for Taiwan's success is the operation of the free market. In recent years, Robert Wade and others have effectively championed the idea that Taiwan's success is due in large measure to effective government industrial planning. These policies are in large measure analogous to those of South Korea, though the industrial base of Taiwan is in small firms and that of Korea in large firms. (See the case study of South Korea.)

Taiwan has had active industrial policy systems in place to license exports, control direct foreign investment both to and from Taiwan, establish export cartels, and to provide fiscal incentives for investment in priority sectors and concessional credit for favored industries.

Taiwan's economic history began with a very highly dirigiste, or state-directed, import substitution-oriented industrialization, in the 1949-1950 period. The 1958 reforms switched intervention to export promotion and introduced market forces. But what emerged was far from a free market--only a less thoroughly planned one. In Taiwan until recently, all imports and exports have had to be covered by a license. Imports are classified into "prohibited," "controlled," and "permissible." Controlled goods include luxuries and some goods produced locally with reasonable quality, in sufficient quantities, and whose prices are not more than a narrow margin (about 5%) above comparable import prices. Even the "permissible" items are subject to strong controls, such as with garments, which until 1980 could only be imported from Europe and America--the least competitive sources. Other goods subject to "competitive origin restrictions" have included yarns, artificial fibers, fabrics, some processed foodstuffs, chemicals, machinery and electrical apparatus. Since the controlled list is larger than the published one, not all "permissibles" are automatically approved. As Robert Wade shows, a potential importer of an item on the hidden list has been asked to provide evidence that domestic suppliers cannot meet foreign price, quality, and timing-of-delivery terms. Wade presents evidence that their function is to jump-start growth industries by providing domestic demand for products targeted by government. Then aggressive incentives are provided for these companies to begin to export these products.

Wade's interpretation for the relative success of this import substitution program, however, is consistent with an emphasis on market incentives. He argues that because it controls quantities of foreign goods entering the local economy, the government can use international prices to discipline the price-setting behavior of protected domestic producers. The government demands to know good reasons why domestic prices of protected items are significantly higher than international prices, especially in the case of inputs to be used for export production. In this way domestic prices for controlled goods can be kept near world price levels, even without free trade of goods across national borders. Wade concludes that an effective government threat of allowing in more goods can itself be sufficient to hold prices down, despite the current trade protection. Wade's argument can be interpreted as analogous to the theory that monopolists will keep prices low to the extent that they fear the entry of a rival firm seeking to take advantage of a prevailing high price in an industry. Thus the argument is that government is able to play an active role in industrial planning without compromising the vitality of market incentives.

Free market incentives. Claims that an economy's success is due to government industrial policies, rather than the action of the free market, are impossible to fully prove. There is always the danger of corruption and inefficiency when government is excessively involved in the economy. Some anti-interventionist economists have gone so far as to argue that Taiwan would have done even better without its industrial policies, part of their contention that "government failure" is almost always worse than market failure in developing countries. This is a difficult position to defend, given that no economies have ever done better.

At the same time, while entrepreneurial dynamism is hard to measure precisely, it is plain for all to see throughout the island. Taiwan is a case in which incentives to produce wealth rather than merely to seek a share of existing wealth ("rent-seeking behavior"), are established with solid property rights and not significantly undermined by other policies.

And certainly, the government of Taiwan has not always been a highly efficient engine of progress. There would seem to be plenty of room for inefficiency merely from the fact that the Republic of China is in the unique situation of administering both a central and a provincial government covering exactly the same territory. This is a legacy of the Chinese civil war, which Taiwan's governing Kuomintang lost. Moreover, until 1991, the government ruled Taiwan under martial law. This would seem to have offered ample opportunities for corruption. Indeed, in 1993, new corruption scandals seem to be reported almost daily in Taiwan's many independent newspapers.

Listening to Taiwan's government and opposition leaders, one might conclude that there are not only two Chinas, but two Taiwans. One is clean, efficient, has a free press, and is democratic. The other is corrupt, inefficient, features government control of television and democratic institutions that are little more than a figleaf over Kuomintang dictatorship. The truth about the government role lies somewhere in between. Taiwan is best understood as a case in which the dynamism of the marketplace is sustained and harnessed with a generally though not universally effective role of government in correcting market failure and promoting sustainable development. Taiwan might indeed have done better if government activities had been scaled back in some fields--but on net there is little doubt that its industrial policies have helped more than hurt. The reverse is true of many other developing countries and it is difficult to draw general conclusions. Of course, now that Taiwan is approaching developed country status, earlier government economic policies may no longer be applicable. The emergence of an effective opposition in the independent-minded Democratic Progressive Party is a factor keeping government failure in check.

Other factors. The other explanations listed earlier were also somewhat important, but are unlikely to have been critical given the decisive role of the seven factors just discussed. They are also special features which other economies cannot easily encourage through policy measures. The 1960s Vietnam War boom affected countries such as the Philippines as much if not more, but without lasting effect; this suggests that other conditions were more important in Taiwan's success. American aid to Egypt has been far larger, and substantially used for investment purposes, but with less impressive results. Undoubtedly the work ethic and attitudes of the labor force were important. At the same time, they could not be called into play without the right incentives being in place, and without the availability of economically productive ideas. At the same time, a work ethic can be stimulated by the right incentives. A long history as an entrepreneurial culture may also be important, but in the long term these will similarly be influenced by incentives for entrepreneurship.

The fact that Taiwan benefitted from beginning export-led growth in the early 1960s, a time of unequaled world growth and a wide-open American market, was an undoubted advantage. On the other hand, other countries such as Thailand have successfully grown through manufactures exports in the 1980s, despite far slower U.S. and world income and trade growth rates. Export-oriented Guangdong province of China is growing far faster in the 1990s than Taiwan ever did, despite continued sluggish world trade growth. The idea that local islanders had little opportunities outside of entrepreneurship has not been proven; in any case, Taiwan seems hardly to differ in this regard from the situation under many other authoritarian regimes around the developing world which have suffered negative per capita income growth.

As to the necessity of economic development as a defense strategy, one can hardly single out Taiwan. The United States guaranteed Taiwan's defense after President Truman sealed off the island in 1950, in response to the Korean crisis. Other developing countries lacking the natural defenses of an island, which are gravely threatened by hostile neighbors have made little development progress in the same period. Military necessity more often represents a diversion of resources needed for development than a productive stimulus.

Conclusion. It seems that Taiwan's stellar success is best explained by a combination of emphasis on education, absorption of productive ideas from abroad, extensive infrastructure development, thoroughgoing land reform, very high rates of savings and investment, effective industrial policy, and last but not least, ensuring that incentives of the marketplace to produce wealth rather than seek a share of existing wealth are established with solid property rights and not undermined by other policies.

Today, Taiwan seems well-characterized by Walt Rostow's notion of an economy in a "drive to maturity," in which the range of the world's most advanced technology and skills are mastered. Government is focussing on collaborating with the private sector on more advanced R&D, as Taiwan moves into high technology fields. In 1991, a huge $300-billion-plus infrastructure development project was announced as part of the ambitious 1991-96 Development Plan, designed to propel Taiwan into the ranks of the developed economies. The education system is being expanded; and universal health insurance is to be in place by 1994. In 1993, however, the infrastructure projects had to be scaled back by about two-thirds, due to tax collection shortfalls. The private sector is being encouraged through incentives and exhortation to take up the slack, but it is unlikely that it can fully do so. Only time will tell how soon Taiwan can reach the status of a fully developed economy.

Are there any drawbacks to Taiwan's growth? Certainly environmental considerations have taken a backseat to economic growth until very recently. Taipei suffers from exceedingly noxious air pollution, for example. Despite a nominal beginning at land use planning, a driver down the island's West coast will find a dizzying jumble of various agricultural, industrial, commercial and residential uses, defying any economic rationale, let alone land use aesthetics. She will find industrial sites perched on landfill over rice paddies and prawn pools, into which some waste products inevitably seep. Attention is given to matters such as endangered species only after much Western pressure has been applied. Even then, as one Taiwan official put it, "the private sector is flexible and vibrant in Taiwan--where there is profit, there is activity."

Moreover, GNP per capita, measured in U.S. dollars, often understates a country's real living levels, since equivalent personal services, from haircuts to advanced training courses, cost so much less. To compensate, adjustments are made to what is termed purchasing power parity. A few countries, such as Japan, have their living standards overstated when incomes are expressed in dollars. Taiwan is also almost certainly such a case; for example its distribution system is biased against consumers in a way very similar to that of Japan. But because the economy does not appear in United Nations and World Bank reports, agencies in which only the Peoples' Republic of China is represented, purchasing power parity estimates comparable to other countries are not readily available. But Taiwan's purchasing power parity income level is likely closer to $7500 than $10,000.

Housing remains small and basic in Taiwan; and motorbikes outnumber cars, a large fraction of which are taxis. (Some of this may be due to incentives of the tax code). Left behind by the miracle, homeless derelicts can be seen sleeping on the streets of

Taipei and Kaohsiung--though these cities differ little in this regard from New York and Washington. With the opening of China, many Taiwan companies are moving lock, stock, and barrel to the mainland; and fears of the hollowing out of the economy, such as has been seen in the U.S. and U.K., are being voiced. But this is likely to bring as much opportunity as problems. And even with such caveats, Taiwan has come exceptionally far; the caveats only qualify Taiwan's success, and point to some necessary future directions; they do not in any way negate its impressive accomplishments.

In sum, Taiwan illustrates well the complex mix of factors behind the kind of rapid economic and social progress often termed a development miracle. The factors which stood out were education, infrastructure, land reform, high savings and investment, absorption of commercial ideas, effective industrial policy and market incentives.

Sources. Due to Taiwan's peculiar status as a non-member of the United Nations and the World Bank, little authoritative scholarly work is available. This study is based largely on government documents, interviews of the author with government and opposition leaders, and other firsthand observations. In addition: Robert Wade, Governing the Market, Princeton Univ. Press, 1991; Alice Amsden, "Taiwan's Economic History: A Case of Etatisme and a Challenge to Dependency Theory," Modern China, 5, 341-80, 1979; Alice Amsden, "Taiwan," Special Issue: Exports of Technology by Newly Industrializing Economies, World Development, 12, 5/6, 1984; Bela Balassa, "The Lessons of East Asian Development: An Overview," Economic Development and Cultural Change, 36, Supplement, S273-290, 1988; Michael Borus and Denis Fred Simon, "High Technology in the Pacific Basin: Analysis and Policy Implications," paper presented at the State Department-NAS Conference on Foreign Competition in Science and Technology, National Academy of Science, May 11, 1989; C.I. Bradford, "Trade and Structural Change, NICs and Next-Tier NICs as Transitional Economies," World Development, 15, 299-316, 1987; Hollis Chenery, Sherman Robinson and Moses Syrquin, Industrialization and Growth: A Comparative Study, New York: Oxford, 1986; Wan-Wen Chu, "Export Led Growth and Import Dependence, the Case of Taiwan 1969-1981," Journal of Development Economics, 28, 265-276, 1988; William Cline, "Can the East Asian Model of Development Be Generalized?" World Development, 10, 81-90, 1982; Carl J. Dahlman, Bruce Ross-Larson and Larry E. Westphal, "Managing Technical Development: Lessons from the Newly Industrializing Countries," World Development, 15, 759-75, 1987; Steffan Jacobsson, "Technical Change and Industrial Policy: The Case of Computer Numerically Controlled Lathes in Argentina, Korea and Taiwan," World Development, 10, 991-1014, 1982; Donald B. Keesing, The Four Successful Exceptions. Official Export Promotion and Support for Export Marketing in Korea, Hong Kong, Singapore and Taiwan, China, UNDP-World Bank Trade Expansion Program Occasional Paper 2, 1988; Deepak Lal, The Poverty of Development Economics, London: Hobart, 1984; Howard Pack and Larry Westphal, "Industrial Strategy and Technological Change: Theory versus Reality," Journal of Development Economics, 22, 87-128, 1986; Robert Wade, "The Role of Government in Overcoming Market Failure: Taiwan, Republic of Korea and Japan," in Helen Hughes, ed., Achieving Industrialization in East Asia, New York: Cambridge University Press, 1988; Robert Wade, "State Intervention in 'Outward-looking' Development: Neoclassical Theory and Taiwanese Practice," in Gordon White, ed., Developmental States in East Asia, New York: St. Martins, 1988; Stephen C. Smith, Industrial Policy in Developing Countries: Reconsidering the Real Sources of Export-Led Growth, Washington: Economic Policy Institute, 1991.

2. Zaire: Immiseration amidst riches; with the counterpoint of Botswana

The state has a vital role in economic development, building education and skills, health, infrastructure and offering guidance in industrial development. When the state plays a healthy role it can improve economic development outcomes. But when civil servants are corrupt, when policy is made for private gain, when political power of top leaders is abused, the state can also make development prospects worse than if it played no role at all.

Zaire is one of the most tragic stories of economic development in the Third World, where a country among the best endowed in natural resources in the world has been devastated by government corruption. In the midst of largely unexploited riches nearly 40 million Zairians are not only among the poorest people in the world--12th poorest among countries with one million or more population according to the World Bank--they are steadily getting poorer. The economy is in a state of total collapse almost impossible to convey with statistics alone.

Zaire is a country which has been estimated to have enough arable land to feed the entire continent of Africa and enough hydro power to provide for all of Africa's electricity, in which food production is declining and industry has ground to a complete halt. The case of Zaire demonstrates that "political development" is a necessary condition for modern economic development. It provides a vivid reminder of just how bad things can get in a developing country even in the mid-1990s. In extreme form, Zaire also illustrates the unfortunate legacy of the Cold War for development in Africa.

Zaire came into independence from Belgium in 1960 with a heavy baggage of oppressive colonial experience. Once called the Belgian Congo, this huge country, almost as large as the United States east of the Mississippi, was long the private personal possession of the Belgian King Leopold. For decades the Belgians governed the colony essentially as a private profit-making business venture, operating mines under virtually slave-like conditions and giving little attention to development needs until the very end of the colonial period. Only after World War II did Belgium begin to make significant efforts on behalf of the development of its colony.

This colonial experience fostered an understandably antagonistic attitude toward government, that sadly carried over from colonial times to the cynical, rapacious attitudes toward government and public service that have prevailed in the post-independence period. This kind of carry-over from conflict with harsh colonial administrations to perceptions of the state as a means of self-aggrandizement is seen in many African countries and is one of the most bitter fruits of the colonial legacy. But perhaps nowhere is this legacy more bitter than in Zaire.

Zaire has been ruled for nearly three decades by the dictator President Mobutu Sese Seko Kuku Mgbendu Wa za Banga. Born Mobutu Joseph Desire, his current official name is translated as "the all-powerful warrior who because of his endurance and inflexible will to win will go from conquest to conquest leaving fire in his wake." In his pictures he is always seen in a trademark leopardskin cap.

Mobutu also changed the country's name, from Congo to Zaire in 1971, in a symbolic show of cutting ties with the colonial past. But Mobutu, who was an accounting clerk in the colonial army, has himself run the country in a way reminiscent of King Leopold. Under Mobutu, Zaire has often been described as a "kleptocracy," a government of theft: a nation run of, by, and for thieves. Mobutu himself is believed to have stolen well over $1 billion and squandered public funds on personal projects.

As Lucy Komisar notes, bribes are considered part of the normal pay of anyone with any authority. Police arrest passersby at random, extorting money. Schoolteachers sometimes demand bribes before they release grades. Hospital guards demand bribes before admitting sick patients. As Joe Davidson of the Wall Street Journal observed, men and women in uniform shamelessly compete for payoffs at the ferry dock. The pervasiveness of such naked corruption is universally attested to by visitors.

Despite the base corruption, political repression and human rights violations of Mobutu's regime, he was generally supported by Western Europe and the United States as a Cold War buffer. Mobutu seized power with CIA backing in 1965, installed to thwart possible Soviet influence on a left-wing regime. The United States alone provided Zaire with over $1 billion in aid in the 1970s and 1980s. When the Cold War ended, this disagreeable marriage of convenience resulted in an abrupt separation, if not quite divorce.

Mobutu attempted to get away with a partial and insincere democratization, having his representatives meet with opposition leaders in a "national political conference." Things did not go the way Mobutu had expected, and his long-time rival Etienne Tshisekedi was selected as transitional prime minister by a coalition of generally pro-democratic, but often ethnically-based, partisan forces. There are some 200 ethnic groups in Zaire.

But this turn of events has only eroded, not eliminated the domination of Mobutu, who still claims the title of president. Western countries thought he should be allowed to remain in power until a transfer of power had been completed to control the army, which at least in retrospect was a complete misreading of the realities of the country. Mobutu no longer tries to run the government from Kinshasa. For some time his official Kinshasa headquarters was moved to his yacht on the Congo River to ensure his safety.

Mobutu is now based securely in his marble jungle palace at Gbadolite, deep in the "interior" of the country. Gbadolite is one of eleven palaces he has built for himself with public money. He enforces his will in the capital through his personal army, the Special Presidential Guard, drawn from his Ngbandi ethnic group. The Guard often operates incognito, without the slightest regard for human rights. Dissenters are murdered, or their children are. Prisoners are starving in the jails, where there is no food to feed them.

Mobutu continues to control the country's treasury, which he is said to treat as his private purse. He also controls the television and radio system, surrounded by loyal Special Presidential Guards, from which he broadcasts fictitious images of an active presidency from his Gbadolite palace. While these broadcasts are ignored in Kinshasa, they look real in the vast country's villages, and help him maintain power.

Mobutu tried to dismiss Interim Prime Minister Tshisekedi in December 1992, but the result has been a standoff. Lacking real power, Tshisekedi's government has been regarded as virtually as fictitious as Mobutu's.

In early 1993, Tshisekedi declared illegitimate Mobutu's new 5-million-zaire note, worth about $1.75 at that time. The army, which had just been paid in these notes, rioted for the third time in as many years. The French ambassador was shot during these riots while observing them from his window. France, the United States, and Belgium formally demanded that Mobutu relinquish authority to Tshisekedi's interim government.

Ethnic conflicts are often complex and fueled by passionate historic hatreds, as we have seen vividly in recent years in the former Yugoslavia. Opportunistic behaviors can be reinforced by ethnic hatreds. Dictators like Milosevic in Serbia--and Mobutu in Zaire--often manipulate ethnic conflict for their own advantage.

For example, in August 1991 after Tshisekedi was elected prime minister, members of the Kasai, an ethnic group based in the center of Zaire, were driven from their homes in Shaba province, in the southwest. In Shaba Tshisekedi was perceived less as a reformer than as a member of the hated Kasai ethnic group. Rather than celebrate discretely, as might have been more prudent, resident Kasai conducted boisterous street celebrations. Shaba's governor, Kyunguwa Kumwanza, had publicly denounced the Kasai "insects," further fanning the flames of ethnic hostility. Mobs made up of the Katangan ethnic group staged bloody ethnic attacks, which local police did nothing to stop, and Mobutu implicitly encouraged. The Kasai fled the area, with hundreds of refugees dying of starvation. Some 60,000 live in a tent city where they would starve if not for the efforts of relief agencies. The Katangans, native to Shaba province, where much of the mineral wealth is located, have long felt exploited by the rest of the country.

In the wake of the fighting, many Western businesses also left the country, taking with them capital and expertise. By early 1993, a general evacuation of Westerners was under way. The signs of economic decay are visible everywhere. Import substitution factories, intended to manufacture locally what had been imported, and viewed as embodying Zaire's future when mineral resources are no longer able to fuel development, have been pillaged and plundered, and finally abandoned, since an earlier outburst of looting and arson that began when soldiers mutinied over lack of pay in September 1991. Even the walls and roofs of factories were stolen. Years of painstaking growth of the modern sector were destroyed overnight, costing close to 100,000 jobs in the Kinshasa area alone. For example, the General Motors assembly plant in Kinshasa suffered so many waves of looters that all that remains is a structural skeleton bearing the GM logo.

Once vibrant copper and cobalt mines in Shaba province and elsewhere are now flooded with water. One historical irony is that Congo, a smaller country north of Zaire, and long shunned by the U.S. as a Marxist regime, is now a growing destination of investment. It is actually considered a more stable and well-governed regime.

Even were Zaire's mines managed honestly and well, commodity riches can be fleeting. There are many international economic pitfalls said to undermine successful reliance on commodities exports as a source of economic development, particularly stressed by structuralist and dependency schools in development.

The development literature has long debated arguments in favor of limiting dependence on primary commodity exporting, thus favoring exports of manufactures. Some development writers have implied that Zaire's problems are rooted in this specialization. The four most important arguments against primary commodity specialization are:

1. Commodity price instability. A very large literature argues that prices of commodities are subject to much larger swings than manufactures and services, and so credit-

constrained less developed countries (LDCs) will suffer foreign exchange earnings instability by specializing in them, likely lowering welfare.

2. Agricultural trade barriers in the developed countries, which tend to be stronger than manufacturing barriers. There have been various "noises" about removing these, but as yet few concrete actions or guarantees of removal.

3. Externalities, linkages, and dynamic effects of specializing in manufactures. Production and export of manufactures has been argued in the development literature to raise average productivity in the economy over time, in part through spinning off positive effects on other sectors. The result may be qualitative technological progress in the economy not easily realized by market forces alone. (These ideas are explored further in Case 14).

4. Declining terms of trade. It has been argued since 1950 by Hans Singer and others that the terms of trade for commodity producers are likely to decline relative to manufactures producers. This is due, among other causes to: downsizing, substitution of new materials (synthetic rubber, fiber optics for cables, etc.), and low income elasticity of demand for these items. The evidence has been somewhat inconclusive, but unfortunately for many of the world's poorest countries, commodity prices resumed their relative downward course with a vengeance in the 1980s, just after large investments in numerous primary commodities were undertaken in Africa, as well as Latin America and South East Asia.

While these arguments are important to consider for development policy, they are certainly not the source of Zaire's problems. With better political development, even a development strategy based exclusively on expansion of such commodities production, and even under the worst scenarios for commodity prices, would lead to a far better situation than Zaire has known in recent years.

By mid-1993, the divided government in Zaire was weaker than ever. With rapid inflation and a plummeting currency, a one million zaire note is now in circulation. Western aid has been largely suspended, though this made little difference for basic needs, since so little of it was getting through to the people who needed it anyway.

What can the outside world do in a case like this? In the case of Zaire there may be no effective option outside military intervention. Sanctions may be of no avail when a ruler is indifferent to the suffering of the country's people, as the world discovered in the case of Sadam Hussein of Iraq. In fact, Mobutu may very well be clinically insane.

Diamonds, a principal export, are a very compact and lightweight commodity, and are easy to smuggle. This makes them the perfect sanctions-breaker.

The entire diamond industry in Zaire is corrupt. Diamond export values are in reality up to twice the officially recorded $185 million for 1992. False transfer pricing in the form of underinvoicing of revenues received from exports is used to avoid taxes and to facilitate capital flight. Senior military officers run protection rackets, skimming a percentage of the diamond exporters' sales.

Mobutu, it has been said, proves that diamonds are a dictator's best friend, and so eventually become a developing nation's burden rather than its boon.

But nearby Botswana shows that mineral wealth can be a benefit in a country with the political development in place. The country offers an instructive counter-point to Zaire. Botswana has had by far the highest rate of growth in sub-Saharan Africa, 8.4% per year over the whole 1965 to 1990 period. In this time Botswana went from being among the very poorest countries in the world to surpass the per capita income of such countries as Turkey and Chile.

The economy of Zaire, in contrast, shrunk at a -2.2% rate throughout this quarter-century period. This is an appropriate period for comparison because Botswana became independent in 1966; and Mobutu came to power in Zaire in 1965.

Botswana's astonishing rate of growth places it higher than any country with more than one million population as reported by the World Bank over this period, including South Korea at 7.1%, Singapore at 6.4% and Hong Kong at 6.1%. The only economy to grow faster than Botswana in this often difficult period is that of Taiwan.

Perhaps even more impressive, unlike its high-growth peers Botswana has been a multi-party democracy, albeit one dominated by a single political party, the Botswana Democratic Party. Elections have been held every five years since 1965. Amnesty International has consistently given Botswana the highest human rights rating in Africa, one higher than the United Kingdom, its former colonial master. There is a free press and no political prisoners. Botswana accomplished these impressive economic and political results while surrounded by white minority regimes (South Africa, Rhodesia and Namibia) for the first half of its history; nearby civil wars have often spilled over into its territory; and a steady stream of refugees has threatened to upset the social order.

There is no doubt that Botswana's diamond wealth has been central to its towering success. Botswana's 16 million metric carat annual diamond production is almost identical with Zaire's 15 million. But Botswana's population is just 1.2 million; Zaire's is much larger at 34.5 million. Zaire has several other important kinds of mineral wealth as well, and though there is no doubt that Botswana's per capita mineral wealth is greater, African countries with strong mineral wealth have typically done worse than those without. Serious scholars of contemporary national development like Michael Porter have argued that absence of natural resources can be a net competitive advantage.

At the same time, this success cannot be attributed only to diamonds. The absence of a dictator like Mobutu has helped also, but even this explanation is not enough. What keeps a country like Botswana from falling prey to a Mobutu? It certainly helps to have a democratic tradition, in which there are pressures to allocate resources to genuine development. What a country spends its wealth on matters, whether that wealth is large or small. Botswana has achieved essentially universal primary education, a rare achievement in the developing world, and a respectable one third of children enroll in secondary education, compared with the sub-Saharan Africa average of under 20%.

Botswana suffered a brutal drought from 1982 to 1987, and poor rural peoples were severely affected. In many countries their plight might have been unattended to until significant starvation began and caught the attention of the world. Botswana built on its social security system and provided relief to the rural poor through a four-pronged system of maintaining food availability, as detailed by Jean Dreze and Amartya Sen: guaranteeing public employment for cash wages which could be spent on available food; direct food distribution to selected groups and agricultural productivity and recovery activities.

Botswana's free press and democratic system seems to be a major factor in this response, as contrasted with the harsh indifference to severe poverty in Zaire. In addition, supporting factors like an absence of glaring inequality and social harmony must also be striven for, as the case of Chile shows. Chile had a long democratic tradition and a history of investing in social development goals like health and education, but this did not prevent its 1973 coup.

On other human development indicators like infant mortality and health professionals per capita, Botswana also scores well. However, the United Nations Development Program (UNDP) Human Development Index ranks the country 94th out of 160, which is 20 points lower than its GNP rank; in other words human development is somewhat lower than predicted by GNP per capita. But if to some degree nonincome measures of development have not quite kept pace with Botswana's astronomical growth rate, its human development performance for Africa is extraordinary. In Sub-Saharan Africa only Gabon rates higher in the UNDP Index (91st); Gabon is a country solidly in the middle per capita income range at the time of its independence, which has grown less than one percent per year since 1965.

Finally, it should be underlined that not all of Botswana's luck has been good; the five year drought of the mid-1980s just described was very harsh by any standards; and other serious droughts such as that of 1979 to 1980 plague the country with some regularity.

A single ethnic group, the Batswana, dominates Botswana; and it is widely considered a development advantage to have a homogeneous population--ranging from political decision-making advantages for selection of public good levels of a population holding similar preferences--to the common historical animosities of neighboring peoples. Minorities often fare poorly in developing--as indeed also often in developed--countries. And in Botswana one of the few blemishes on the development record is that the minority aboriginal bushmen fare much less well than the majority Batswana, though this problem is a very difficult one to remedy. Botswana will continue to bear watching to see if its human development performance can fully catch up with its income growth, but it already demonstrates the good use a country can make of its natural resources when it has an advanced political development to facilitate economic development.

Taken together, the case of immiseration amidst riches in Zaire with the counterpoint of development success in Botswana shows clearly the vital role of political development, and the importance of the role of the state, whether to do good or ill, in economic development.

Sources: The Situation in Zaire, Hearing before the Subcommittee on African Affairs, Washington: Government Printing Office, Nov. 6, 1991; Washington Post, Oct. 10 and Oct. 13, 1991; March 31, 1992; Feb. 23 and April 13, 1993; New York Times, April 30, 1992; March 21, 1993; Wall Street Journal, Dec. 17, 1991; Christian Science Monitor, Feb 5, 1993; Steve Askin, "Zaire's Tyrant Hangs On," Christian Science Monitor, March 9, 1993; The Economist, Jan. 23, 1993; World Bank World Development Report 1986, 1991 and 1992; United Nations Development Program Human Development Report 1992; Lucy Komisar, "The Claws of the Dictatorship in Zaire: The "Leopard" Still Rules," Dissent, Summer 1992; Jean Dreze and Amartya Sen, Hunger and Public Action, Oxford: Clarendon; Michael Porter, Competitive Advantage of Nations (NY: Free Press, 1990); Harvey, Charles and Stephen R. Lewis Jr., Policy Choice and Development Performance in Botswana, New York, St. Martins, 1990; Picard, Louis A., The Politics of Development in Botswana: A Model for Success? Boulder: Rienner, 1987; Stedman, Stephen J., ed., Botswana: The Political Economy of Democratic Development (especially the chapter by Stephen R. Lewis), Boulder: Rienner, 1993; Robert Klitgaard, Tropical Gangsters, New York: Basic Books, 1990; and other personal communications.

3. The Bangladesh Food for Work Program (FFWP)

Success in the struggle against poverty must begin in the countryside. However important the role of industrialization for growth, rural development remains a vital condition for development success. Agriculture remains important for the foods, raw materials, and export earnings it provides. Moreover, about three-quarters of the world's absolutely poor are found in rural areas. This fact often surprises travelers whose experience of developing countries is largely limited to tourist attractions, and to cities where people often look poor but are more likely to be receiving minimum levels of nutrition and other basic needs than their counterparts in rural areas. Rural poverty leads to rapid population growth and excess migration to the cities. It puts great stress on the environment, as those faced with starvation will get what income they can from their land without regard for the effect of their practices on the land. A "vicious cycle" often results, in which the poor are effectively forced to take actions which keep them poor in future periods.

Infrastructure development plays a vital role in achieving rural progress. Many rural areas in poor countries are still without road links to the outside world or lack access to nearby market towns. Communication links may be few, and irrigation nil. But with low levels of nutrition, productivity of laborers is also low. Infrastructure thus conditions rural development through its impact on the various rural markets, and on the health and education of the rural poor.

Bangladesh, like many developing countries, has been seeking strategies for tackling this cluster of rural development problems. With a GNP per capita of just $210, Bangladesh is the 10th poorest country in the world among those with at least 1 million citizens. Like many poor countries, it seeks both growth and poverty alleviation. But poverty is so severe--85% are absolutely poor according to UN statistics--that the country can hardly wait for the benefits of modern sector growth to eventually trickle down to the poor. At the same time, the country does not wish to sacrifice future growth by its care for the poor today.

Entitlement transfer programs can stifle incentives for work and divert public funds away from needed infrastructure investments. They can also be very wasteful in that much of the benefits go to the nonpoor and many of the poor get no benefits. General food and other subsidies end up benefitting many nonpoor people, who also receive cheaper food and other goods, while missing many of the poor who grow and forage what they can. Successful "means-testing" of poverty programs, or screening program beneficiaries to make sure they are really poor, is very costly--if not impossible to achieve. This not only wastes money on administration, but errors will inevitably be made, and corruption by public officials all too commonly destroys the program.

Bangladesh thinks it has found a solution that will help it respond to several problems at once--infrastructure needs, poverty and the counterproductive incentives and secondary effects created by many poverty programs.

The Food for Work Program (FFWP) FFWP was begun in 1974. The FFWP organizes and pays with food for construction and maintenance of agriculture-supporting infrastructure: mainly irrigation, drainage and embankment works, and roads, during the slack agricultural season of December through April. The allocation of food to the program has increased steadily over the years and the program now generates about 100 million days of employment each year. The World Bank estimates that at least 17 extra days of employment are generated for each landless laborer in Bangladesh in construction alone.

Unlike poverty programs in most developing countries, the FFWP really reaches the poor rather than subsidizing everyone or even disproportionately favoring the more affluent. The basic reason is that an incentive for self-selection is built into the program. Few non-poor persons can be expected to choose to work in labor intensive construction all day for pay in basic foodstuffs, a conjecture strongly supported by the available evidence. Such programs always have opportunity costs to the poor; and most participants must give up some farm or nonfarm self-employment work time to participate.

But the evidence is that net gains to the poor remain substantial. There is some attention, though probably not enough, to making the program fit an appropriate seasonal pattern. That is, to have work available through the program when demand for agricultural labor is at its lowest levels in the crop cycles. The need for the program is smaller when agricultural labor demand is higher. Since government-financed labor-intensive construction is probably not a permanent solution to poverty, it is very important to avoid making the program work-replacing rather than work-creating.

The program also benefits rural development, including poor farmers, by producing valuable infrastructure. Moreover, it avoids the reductions in the incentive to work, or moral hazard, caused by some welfare programs. With distribution to the poor concentrated in one place, it is easier to monitor for corruption. Private voluntary organizations such as CARE play an important monitoring role, making sure projects meet development goals as well as sound engineering standards, and observing pay rates actually paid to laborers. Environmental sustainability is an important new project criteria; and the program has begun to incorporate afforestation schemes. The Food for Work Program compares favorably with an irrigation project financed by the World Bank in the 1970s that mostly benefitted well-off farmers.

The distribution of land is highly unequal in Bangladesh, yet it is still better than in many other developing countries. The benefits of the infrastructure created are thus more widely disbursed, though still biased in favor of the larger farmers.

Better land distribution is needed in Bangladesh. Small farmers frequently lose their land to constantly shifting river patterns. As new lands are opened up by these changes, these are supposed to be distributed to those who have lost land. But often local powerful landlords, who control local political machines--and enforce their will with armed paid thugs--take this land for themselves, hiring the poor as sharecroppers. Clamping down on such activities would help ensure that the benefits of the program are better distributed.

This is not a program that works only in one country. For example, Maharashtra state in India has long operated a similar program that has received high marks in independent evaluations. That program has been expanded and is working well in several parts of India.

Development economists cannot design poverty policy based purely on economic theory and divorced from the politics of support for taxation and expenditure for various alternative programs. An added dimension of FFWPs is that it seems easier to ensure political support for this program than for other poverty programs. Since it is available to anyone who requests it, nonpoor people who fear that they may become poor in the future will be more likely to support it as a kind of unemployment insurance, or insurance against crop failure. This in turn may encourage poor farmers to take reasonable risks that substantially increase expected farm output but that would otherwise be perceived as too dangerous because of their small savings. More affluent people tend to be more generous with income maintenance policies if they know the poor will have to work to receive benefits. They are more likely to support it if they think they will also receive economic benefits themselves, and infrastructure fits this bill well.

Some of the best evidence of the effectiveness of the Food for Work Program in targeting the poorest of the poor comes from household surveys conducted by the International Food Policy Research Institute (IFPRI) in Washington in conjunction with the Bangladesh Institute of Development Studies (BIDS) in Dhaka. Samples were taken in over 30 locations within walking distance of FFWP construction sites throughout the country. Sites were divided by a number of criteria among "more developed" and "less developed" villages.

One finding is that the infrastructure the projects have created has led to significant gains in output and to the incomes of the poor. Infrastructure endowment is associated with 24% increases in agricultural income, 78% increases in livestock and fisheries income, and a doubling of wages; while business and industry income increases a much more modest 17%. Moreover, the landless and functionally landless farmers get a larger share of these increases in wages, and in agricultural, livestock and fisheries income, while the more modest business and industry income gains accrue to large landowners. Thus, overall, the distributional impact of rural infrastructure is very favorable.

Another important finding is that in villages endowed with infrastructure, participation in the labor force increases; and a large part of this represents increased labor supply by women. In developing countries, such changes generally raise womens' effective income and status, while lowering birth rates, and lead to better nutrition for children.

The IFPRI-BIDS survey showed that infrastructure has important effects on the composition of employment. Development of infrastructure creates opportunities for nonfarm employment, where productivity and incomes are higher at the same time as the work is less arduous. Those in villages with developed infrastructure sell more of their output and buy more of the food and other products they need, so that villagers can benefit from a more efficient division of labor. Infrastructure also leads to a shift to voluntary wage employment, from low-productivity self-employment in informal sector activities. This shift increases average annual incomes. Unquestionably, these changes mean that traditional lifestyles are altered, and this may have some drawbacks. But the net result is that infrastructure helps reduce poverty, and villagers jump at the opportunities that it provides them.

Further analysis of these data done for the World Bank by Martin Ravallion confirms the overwhelming concentration of participants in the program among the poorest of Bangladeshis; and almost all participants would be considered poor even by local standards. Using the village data survey and other data Ravallion estimated that 60% of the participants in the FFWP came from the poorest quartile of rural households.

The existence of the FFWP probably put upward pressure on wages or otherwise increased the credibility of sharecroppers in their bargaining with landlords. This is important for improving the wellbeing of poor tenant sharecroppers because under the system of sharecropping under assumptions reasonable for South Asia the landlord can often force tenants to their "reservation utility levels" despite the presence of regulations intended to help sharecroppers. Not all the income received from the program represents net gains for participants. The poor must give up informal sector work and work time on their own farm plots to participate. The evidence as a whole suggests that these opportunity costs of participation represent about half of the value of food received from working in the program.

A Food for Work Program is not sufficient for alleviation of poverty. Needed infrastructure work may not be in the vicinity of the poor, and make-work is costly. Some of the poorest of the poor may be too weak to come to work. There is no guarantee that the men who work on these projects will give an adequate share of the food to their wives and children; and orphans and others may simply have no family member who can or will participate. Corruption, such as skimming, overstating work done, and underpayment of participants, has not been (and probably cannot be) entirely prevented. Some roads have washed away, perhaps avoidably with better engineering practices. The FFWP has also been criticized for lack of integration with other important local rural development schemes, though this is thought to be improving. Thus Food for Work Programs have some limitations and must be complemented with other poverty programs.

But in a world of uncertainty about who are the poor, moral hazard over incentives to work, and the politics of program support, a program like the FFWP is one of the best places for a low-income country to start.

Sources: Martin Ravallion, Reaching the Poor through Rural Public Employment, World Bank Discussion Paper 94, 1990; Food for Work Program, Special Issue of Bangladesh Development Studies, Vol. 11, 1-235, 1983; Raisuddin Ahmed and Mahabub Hossain, Developmental Impact of Rural Infrastructure in Bangladesh, Washington: International Food Policy Research Institute with Bangladesh Institute of Development Studies, 1990; Frances Stewart, Basic Needs in Developing Countries (1985); Inderjit Singh, The Great Ascent: The Rural Poor in South Asia, Johns Hopkins, for the World Bank, 1990;

4. Sharecropping and Constraints on Agrarian Reform: India

In developing countries, one of the most common forms of farm tenant contracts is called sharecropping, in which the tenant farmer uses some of the landowner's farmland in exchange for a share of food output, such as half the rice grown. The landlord's share may vary from less than a third to more than two-thirds of output, depending on local labor availability, and the other inputs (such as seeds and hoes) that the landlord provides. In this case study some of the principal economic perspectives on sharecropping will be reviewed; then we will look at the case of India, where sharecropping is widespread. For convenience in this case study unless otherwise noted we will assume that output is split 50-50 between landlord and sharecropper, the most common type of sharecropping in practice.

Sharecropping was long considered by economists to be economically inefficient. Alfred Marshall observed that the farmer was in effect paid only part, rather than all, of his marginal product, and would rationally reduce work effort accordingly. With 50-50 sharing, the sharecropper has an incentive to work until only half of his marginal product of labor is equal to his alternative wage (or other opportunity cost of his time). But more recent work by Cheung, Newbery, Stiglitz and others suggests that sharecropping may be at least relatively efficient after all, in that it makes the best out of an inherently uncertain and risky situation for both landlord and tenant.

In an influential analysis, S.N.S. Cheung argued that Marshall's pessimistic conclusion about sharecropping is flawed. First, Cheung noted that Marshall's model takes the share parameter as fixed when rationally it should be set as a result of negotiation. Second, Cheung noted that Marshall's model leaves the tenant free to decide on his level of effort, when rationally the landlord should demand and enforce a high effort. Cheung showed with a theoretical model that if the landlord can pick both share and effort then a level of output can be induced that just equals the values that would result under a pure land rent contract, in which a fixed rent is paid for the use of the land regardless of how much is ultimately grown.

But Cheung's result has been widely doubted on the realistic grounds that landlords are almost never in a position to fully dictate effort levels of tenants, at least not without incurring substantial supervision costs. The landlord's farms are often widely dispersed across several tenants in many different locations some distance from the village. The landlord or a hired supervisor would have to visit various tenants on various farm plots to monitor their effort. Tenants would know they stand a good chance of not being monitored at any one time. Moreover tenants often have advance notice that the landlord or supervisor is coming to their place of work--if only by the noise or dust cloud caused by an approaching wagon or motor vehicle. And it is simply too costly to have a supervisor watch a farmworker at all times. Finally, supervisors must themselves be monitored to make sure they are doing the overseeing work they are supposed to, and though landlords will spend some time monitoring the work of supervisors and farmworkers, they often have too high an opportunity cost of time to spend very large amounts of time their own in supervision tasks.

But Cheung also noted that poor farmers were likely to be risk averse, and several studies such as Fred Boadu's research on cocoa production in Ghana have found some relation between the presence of share contracts and higher risk in output yields. This insight has enabled development economists to take the analysis one step further to the modern theory of sharecropping contracts.

If the landlord pays the tenant a straight wage, which would be efficient if the tenant always gave his full effort and it didn't cost the landlord anything to make sure of this, the tenant has every incentive to accept the money and not work hard. If the tenant pays a straight rent for the land, he faces the appalling risk that there will be a particularly lean year, such as caused by a drought, and there will not be enough food left over after the rent is paid up to prevent starvation. Thus, sharecropping is now understood to represent a compromise between two types of risk: the risk to the landlord that the tenant will not do much work, and the risk to the tenant that a fixed rent will in some years leave him no income. Given high unemployment risk, the tenant may also prefer the certainty of self-employment as a sharecropper. So even though sharecropping would be inefficient in a world of perfect certainty, in the real world it is "as efficient as we can get."

But the economic and social framework in which sharecropping takes place is one of extraordinary social inequality and far-reaching market failure. In many cases, when the peasant faces his landlord, he faces not only the individual whom he must persuade to rent him productive land, but at the same time his prospective employer, his loan officer, and often his ultimate customer for any crops he wishes to sell. These are the conditions known as "interlocking factor markets," and they provide the rural landlord with abundant sources of monopoly and monopsony power, making traditional rural economic and social organization hardily resistant to efforts at reform. The consequences of this have been explored with economic theory and with case studies of agrarian regions.

Suppose a well-meaning government puts a cap on interest rates the landlord can charge. The landlord may simply respond by lowering any or all of the wage rate, the tenant's share of the crop, the price the landlord pays for any crops the tenant seeks to sell; or by raising the implicit price of seeds and tools advanced to the tenant. Under some conditions, in particular, the availability of a perfectly elastic supply of tenants and the ability of the landlord to subdivide his land into as many plots as he chooses, the peasant is forced to the same "reservation utility level," or next-best income opportunity, as before. One feature of this analysis, due to Avishay Braverman and T.N. Srinivasan, is that the peasant's effort per hectare increases with decreases in plot size. Interlinked factor market sharecropping does have the advantage that it is in the landlord's interest to see to it that his sharecropper receives credit from the lowest-cost source. Attempts to regulate several of these interlocked markets at once in an uncertain economy will generally lead to inefficiency--if not leave most tenants unemployed as landlords switch to entirely different uses for their land. But the Braverman and Srinivasan analysis concludes that "nothing short of land reform will affect the tenant's welfare."

As Yujiro Hayami and his collaborators, among others, have argued, well-meaning attempts to improve the lot of peasants by introducing piecemeal reforms, or by "negative" steps such as banning sharecropping, misunderstand the problems and choices facing farm laborers and have sometimes completely backfired in practice. Instead, land reform must not happen in a vacuum, but must first address the peasant's natural aversion to the extraordinary risks of rural poverty. It must offer some means of insurance against weather or price calamities; it must offer training in all aspects of economic life as a farm owner-operator, including not just modern cultivation methods but business, credit management, marketing, and other skills. Otherwise the resulting underuse of capital, fertilizer and similar inputs, and new varieties may result in an outcome much inferior even to sharecropping.

The teaching of basic literacy and numeracy may be a land reform prerequisite. Steps to reduce monopoly powers of landlords without destroying rural employment are needed. A progressive land tax discouraging speculative fallow land holdings, coupled with a ceiling on aggregate land owned, will reduce monopoly power; and will do so with a minimum of interventionist regulations which could backfire. Government will also need to help farmers obtain credit to buy land as it comes on the market. But otherwise, the less specific, discretionary, and interventionist activity of government, the less the actual opportunity for the landholding class to subvert land reform through corrupt practices.

Finally, policy must seek the right individual and group balance between assured family proprietorship on the one hand, and cooperation with other farmers, sometimes with public assistance, on the other. Thus land reform is not an event, but a process, one which may be expected to take up to a full generation.

Share tenancy continues to be extremely widespread in India despite numerous attempts by national and state governments to promote tiller-ownership and legally discourage if not outlaw traditional tenancy arrangements under many circumstances. Under 1952 legislation, a 30-acre limit was placed on traditional landlord (zamindari) landholdings. Tenants can request that land on which they labor be formally registered under the legislation and can eventually obtain title to it. The fact that they often do not may be taken as suggesting that there may be something to the theories that in a world of uncertainty share tenancy brings clear benefits to laborers as well as owners.

On the other hand, the zamindari law was not strictly enforced, nor was it well understood among peasants. There has been the real worry among peasants that until clear title is obtained one has to pay rent to the state--often viewed as operating under rigid and unfeeling bureaucratic rules--rather than a paternalistic landlord; and on net they may actually face greater risk of losing the land. A peasant may worry that if he sought tiller rights on one plot of land, landlords would never give him the opportunity to lease any other land in the future. Moreover, as Pranab Bardhan notes, a peasant is sometimes under "extraeconomic coercion" by landlords and may fear for his physical safety. Finally, a peasant may fear that success at gaining land will bring the opprobrium of all other landless farmers in the village who may (plausibly) consider their own future chance of renting land in the village threatened by the precedent.

Empirical evidence on sharecropping in India has been mixed. In Land Labor and Rural Poverty, Pranab Bardhan reported on a survey of over 300 villages in four Indian states. This survey confirmed that some form of sharecropping was the overwhelmingly predominant form of tenancy in India. It also showed that in practice, there are a very wide variety of forms of sharecropping contracts across regions in India. Within most villages, contracts were of a single type, but in a significant number of villages several contract types were found to coexist. Patterns were sometimes hard to discern, but some did emerge: high-yielding varieties were associated with higher tenant shares; in West Bengal, 50-50 sharecropping was much more common when fertilizer is not used than when it is used; and generally, the tenant's share tended to be higher when the landlord did not share in costs, while a very wide range of patterns of cost-sharing were observed.

Traditionally, the landlord pays land and irrigation taxes and the tenant supplies draft animal and plow. The cost of chemical fertilizer is commonly shared on a 50-50 basis. Close to half of the tenants in each region were found to have taken a production loan from the landlord, with a majority of these paying some form of interest. The tenant is occasionally obligated to perform other services for the landlord, at times without pay. Often this obligation is strictly outside the tenancy contract, and may represent extraeconomic coercion.

One of the most detailed single-village case studies of sharecropping and its connections to other village agricultural activities is Bliss and Stern's Palanpur: The Economy of an Indian Village. Palanpur is a village of mud and brick houses with a population of about 1000 located in Western Uttar Pradesh. Some 22.8% of land in Palanpur is under tenancy; and sharecropping, accounting for about 20% of cultivated land, is its usual form. Unlike the familiar overlord image, many of those renting out land or hiring farm labor own rather small quantities of land. This contrasts with assumptions in theoretical work such as that of Braverman and Srinivasan. Bliss and Stern infer from national statistics that overall some 14.2% of land is under tenancy in India, but there are some reasons to surmise that national statistics understate the actual extent of tenancy.

Most share contracts in Palanpur were found to feature 50-50 output sharing; and full tenant responsibility for traditional costs of seeds, draft animals and cultivation labor, as well as of modern (or "discretionary") costs such as fertilizer and irrigation. This differs from studies of other parts of India which have found that 50-50 sharing of discretionary costs is common. These contract requirements mean that to be qualified as a tenant, a farmer must own or have access to draft animals. In practice, renting draft animal services is almost impossible. Thus a potential sharecropper will not typically be among the absolutely poor. This also helps explain why many less affluent peasants are at constant risk of becoming absolutely poor: a wealth "shock" represented by the death of a draft animal may easily have the effect of pushing a family below the absolute poverty line.

For whatever reasons, the 50-50 output sharing rule has been in force in Palanpur for decades. This means that in Palanpur, market equilibration, or the equating of quantities of supply and demand in labor and land markets, has had to take place through mechanisms other than changes in the sharing rule. For example, Bliss and Stern suggest that disappointed would-be tenants will sell their draft animals or otherwise take themselves out of the market of potential renters--even though they might have been willing to work for a smaller output share if such a contract were available. Of course many other prices and quantities of inputs may vary. In any case we must assume that for some reason landlords and tenants find the 50-50 output sharing rule very convenient. Certainly it is easy to calculate and carries the social offer of being a "fair deal."

Interestingly, modern or discretionary costs must be advanced by the tenant, and half reimbursed by the landlord only at harvest time. As Bliss and Stern note, this standard contract feature gives an incentive to a landowner to rent out land if he can find a tenant with cash or access to credit. At the time that a sharecropping arrangement is initiated, landlord and tenant also must reach agreement on which crops will be grown and which inputs will be used.

In the few exceptions to sharecropping tenancy in Palanpur, a landlord who is often absent from the village, say to perform a salaried job outside of the village, will rent the land on a pure cash basis. This may be a relatively small rent because of the larger resulting risk that the tenant must bear. But this finding is consistent with the view that the landlord must play some, if a limited, monitoring role even under sharecropping rather than wage contracts.

Indeed, Bliss and Stern find that landlords regularly observe the progress of cultivation, and that tenants often complained that landlord interference was onerous. They also argue that legal restrictions on tenancy arrangements in which landlords also play a supervisory role may serve to encourage sharecropping, because it is easier for the landlord to claim he is cultivating the land himself and the tenant is a legal wage employee.

Although Palanpur contracts are for a duration of one season, in practice tenants have an incentive to work harder than this short-term horizon would suggest. In their interviews, Bliss and Stern were often told that landlords prefer a good farmer to a poor one, and surely a tenant's performance in previous seasons will be the key basis on which to judge a farmer's quality. Thus, we may judge that tenants will find it optimal to build up a reputation for quality work; though the reputation theory literature of industrial organization would also suggest that at some point in their working life they will find it optimal to live on their past reputations and work less hard, thereby running their reputations down.

Bliss and Stern also examined efficiency across sharecropped and owner-farmed land. Overall, there is no difference in input use or output efficiency, which corresponds to Cheung's views. Surprisingly, in comparing lands on which a farmer sharecrops some land as well as farms some land he owns himself, sharecropped lands show somewhat greater efficiency. This is a direct test that holds constant the attributes of the cultivator. Bliss and Stern suggest that the sharecropped (landlord owned) lands may be of higher quality than lands individually owned by these sharecroppers. They deemed this plausible because owners are of higher caste than sharecroppers. A seemingly statistically significant result may also have been found by chance. In any case, little evidence emerged in their study that sharecropping is truly inefficient as Marshall had expected. But other studies had previously concluded otherwise: For example, comparing sharecropped and other land in Northeast India tilled by the same farmer, Clive Bell found that the sharecropped land had lower yields, though this difference was generally not statistically significant.

Sheila Bhalla found some evidence in support of the idea that landlords manipulate contract terms to push laborers to their reservation utility. She found large variations in the terms of the sharecropping contract, including the output shares themselves.

One of the most advanced multi-village econometric studies of sharecropping was recently conducted by Radwan Ali Shaban using data from four districts in semi-arid tropical parts of India: Mahbubnagar in Andhra Pradesh, Sholapur and Akola in Maharashtra, and Sabarkantha in Gujarat. Most tenants cultivated at least some land they owned. This study found that both inputs and outputs per unit of land were greater for these tenants on land they owned than on land they sharecropped. Output was almost a third higher on the owned plots; and even after controlling for irrigation, plot value and soil quality output per acre was over 16% higher. With similar controls, family male labor was about 21% higher, family female labor 47% higher and draft animal (bullock) inputs 17% higher on the owned plots. But no statistically significant differences were found in comparing plots that were owned with those that were leased on a fixed-rent basis. And while offering a careful statistical analysis involving more villages and offering more definitive statistical tests, the study did miss some of the detailed observations of peasant behavior from the Palanpur study. Moreover, these findings do not prove that sharecroppers would be better off if they could own or lease on a fixed-rent basis, if they are averse to risk. For now, though, the study must shift the weight of evidence in favor of lower technical efficiency on sharecropped land.

The theory and evidence considered in this study suggests that sharecropping is less technically efficient than owner-farming or fix-rent farming in many, but not all cases. But risk-averse sharecroppers may be better off than if they had to pay a fixed rent or mortgage. There is some evidence that the more backward areas of India such as Bihar conform to the picture of high landlord bargaining power, interlinked contracts, and tenant indebtedness to the landlord; while more advanced areas such as Punjab and Haryana show essentially modern landlord-tenant relationships. Landless laborers are finding it harder to obtain the use of land on the basis of share tenancy.

In any case, the complexity of the issues and the lack of consistency in the data suggest that the case for land reform is on more solid ground if it rests on inefficiencies of very small farms and perhaps of very large ones--and on its anti-poverty and distributional advantages, making the use of land possible for landless laborers--rather than the inefficiency of sharecropping contracts themselves. Given the tenacity of landlord power and traditional contract practices, and the natural risk aversion of poor peasants, outlawing particular forms of tenancy such as sharecropping as a response to efficiency and equity problems is likely to be counterproductive as a policy for alleviating poverty.

Sources. Pranab K. Bardhan, Land Labor and Rural Poverty, New Delhi: Oxford (1984); S.N.S. Cheung, The Theory of Share Tenancy, Univ. of Chicago Press, 1969, J.E. Stiglitz, "Incentives and Risk Sharing in Sharecropping," Review of Economic Studies, April 1974; and D.M.G. Newberry, "Risk-sharing, Sharecropping and Uncertain Labor Markets," Review of Economic Studies, Oct. 1977; Braverman, Avishay and T.N. Srinivasan, "Agrarian Reforms in Developing Rural Economies Characterized by Interlinked Credit and Tenancy Markets," in Hans Binswanger and Mark Rosenzweig, eds., Contractual Arrangements, Employment and Wages in Rural Labor Markets in Asia, New Haven: Yale (1984); Radwan Ali Shaban, "Testing between Alternative Models of Sharecropping," Journal of Political Economy, 95, 5, 893-920 (1987); Yujiro Hayami et al, Toward an Alternative Land Reform Paradigm, A Philippine Perspective, Manila, Ateneo de Manila University Press, 1990; C.J. Bliss and N.H. Stern, Palanpur: The Economy of an Indian Village, Oxford: 1982; Sheila Bhalla, Economic and Political Weekly, 1976 and 1983; Boadu, Fred O., "The Efficiency of Share Contracts in Ghana's Cocoa Industry, J. of Development Studies, 29, 1, 108-120 Oct. 1992; Jean P. Dreze and Anandita Mukherjee, "Labor Contracts in Rural India: Theory and Evidence," in S. Chakravarty (ed.) The Balance Between Industry and Agriculture in Economic Development, vol. III; Clive Bell, "Alternative Theories of Sharecropping: Some Tests using Evidence from Northeast India," Journal of Development Studies, 317-346, July, 1977.

5. Hope for the Rural Poor: The Grameen Bank of Bangladesh

One of the biggest problems facing the poor is access to credit. For the poor urban peddler, access to credit can mean a chance to build a bigger inventory, so she has items on hand when customers request them, and can eventually move from the insecurity of being a petty street hawker to the stability of being a established vendor. For the poor rural peasant access to credit can mean a chance to purchase tools, a draft animal, and small capital goods that can enable him to greatly improve his productivity, diversify crops and move toward commercial farming by producing some cash crops for the market, and eventually move from marginal peasant or landless agricultural laborer to established commercial farmer. For the poor rural landless laborer, access to credit can mean a chance to learn skills, purchase raw materials like cloth and tools like a sewing machine, and eventually move from the edge of survival to established business person. The Grameen Bank of Bangladesh is an excellent illustration of how this credit can be provided to those who need it, while minimizing the risk that resources will be wasted.

The Grameen Bank was conceived by Muhammad Yunus a former Chittagong University economics professor, as a private nonprofit development "action and research project." Professor Yunus had become convinced from his research that the lack of access to credit on the part of the poor was a binding constraint on their economic progress. He wanted to demonstrate that it was possible to lend to the poor without collateral, and to determine the best system for doing so.

Professor Yunus began the operation in 1976 with--at least legend has it--a capitalization of just $30. He was able to convince the Bangladesh agricultural development bank (BKB) to provide some initial loan money. The first loans through BKB were guaranteed personally by Professor Yunus. A series of expansions convinced the government of Grameen's value, and the Grameen Bank was formally incorporated under government charter in 1983. The Bank continued to grow very rapidly and now has almost 1000 branch offices throughout the country. The branch office, covering 15 to 20 villages, is the basic organizational unit, and is responsible for its profits and losses.

Since its founding, the public-cooperative Grameen Bank has enabled well over one million poor Bangladeshis, more than three-quarters of them women, most of them landless, to start or upgrade their own small businesses. Borrowers are limited to those who own less than one half acre. Representatives of Grameen branches often go door to door in the villages they cover to inform people, who are generally illiterate and very reticent about dealing with banks, about its services.

Grameen, which alternatively means Rural or Village in the Bengali language, is incorporated as a publicly supported credit union, with borrowers owning 75% of the bank's stock and the government owning the remainder. The bank sets its own policy with strong borrower input, independent of government control. Grameen's annualized interest rate on loans is 16%. This excludes however a 25% surcharge on loan interest amounts that borrowers pay into an insurance Emergency Fund; it has been little used. The average annual inflation rate in Bangladesh has been 9.6% over the 1980-1990 period, making the real interest rate about 7.6%.

Grameen's 16% loans can be compared with traditional moneylenders' loansharking rates of 120 to 200%. These moneylenders generally have a great deal of monopolistic power. Sometimes, though by no means always, they use extraeconomic coercion to get peasants to borrow from them at these high rates of interest and to ensure repayment; built into these moneylenders' rates are such costs as wages for maintaining thugs who enforce the moneylenders' dictates. These rural moneylenders' interest rates are not the result of competitive market forces. True, the traditional system may not be as inefficient as some writers have claimed. Because they are locally based, even though they do not move in the same social circles as low-income borrowers these lenders have access to information about the credit-worthiness of borrowers that would be very hard for traditional banks to obtain. But one of the beauties of the Grameen Bank is that it trumps these moneylenders' informational advantages by using information held by the close peers of the borrowers.

Moreover, Grameen does not just substitute for existing moneylenders. Not only do few Grameen borrowers ever receive loans from formal borrowers, but it has been estimated by Grameen that only about one-fifth are served by the informal lenders. Another two thirds can sometimes get small interest-free loans from relatives or friends. The remainder have no access to any form of credit.

To qualify for uncollateralized loans, potential borrowers form five-member groups. Each member must undergo a two-week training session before any member can secure a loan; and the training sessions are followed up with weekly group meetings with a bank officer. Grameen relies on what could be called the "collateral of peer pressure." Once a member of the group receives a loan, no other member may borrow until a regular repayment record has been established; and no repeat loans are approved until all members' accounts are settled. Members know the characters of group members, and only join groups with members they believe likely to repay their loans.

A significant proportion of new borrowers pay installments in advance, presumably to qualify quickly for a larger loan. The five-person group size was not decided arbitrarily, nor on prior insight, but on the basis of experimentation. Initially, loans were awarded directly to individuals, but this required too much staff time to control the use and repayment of the loan. After the idea of mutual responsibility was developed, large groups of 10 or more were tried at first, but this proved too large for intimate and informal peer to peer monitoring to be effective. Groups of five proved in practice to work best.

Peer oversight has contributed to Grameen's astonishing 98% ultimate repayment rate. By contrast, the country as a whole has a repayment rate of 30 to 40%, and the Industrial Bank of Bangladesh has been infamous for having almost all of its loans to the relatively wealthy in default.

Group members are trained in such practical matters as bank procedures, the group savings program, the role of the center chief and the chairperson of the 5-member group, and even how to write their signatures. In addition, training has a moral component, stressing the Bank's 16 principles, or "Decisions," to be adhered to by each member. These Decisions were formulated in a national conference of 100 female center chiefs in 1984. They emphasize modern values, including self-discipline and hard work, hygiene, refusal to participate in backward practices like demanding bridal dowries, and mutual assistance. Adherence to these principles and attendance at rallies featuring the chanting of the Decisions are not formal requirements for receiving loans but they are said to have become effective, implicit requirements.

Here is a sample from the 16 Decisions: #3- We shall not live in dilapidated houses. We shall repair our houses and work toward constructing new houses as soon as possible. #4- We shall grow vegetables all the year round. We shall eat plenty of them and sell the surplus. #6- We shall plan to keep our families small... #8- We shall always keep our children and the environment clean. #11- We shall not take any dowry in our sons' weddings, neither shall we give any dowry in our daughters' weddings... We shall not practice child marriage. #13- For higher income we shall collectively undertake higher investments.

Much has been written anecdotally about the structure of the Grameen Bank and the beneficial impact it has had on the lives of its members. But most of the solid quantitative information we have of the effects of the Grameen Bank comes from surveys conducted by Mahabub Hossain for the International Food Policy Research Institute.

The group structure facilitates the formation of cooperatives or joint ventures among the participants, encouraging ventures too large or too risky for poor individuals to undertake alone. Grameen also works to facilitate the accumulation of savings among its members through savings requirements or incentives for its borrowers to save. Hossain found that the working capital of borrowers tripled on average within 27 months.

Loans are only made for income-generating activities and have financed a wide range of activities, most of them not based on crop production. Activities financed have included dress (sari) weaving, shoe repair, livestock and poultry raising, small-scale food processing, paddy and rice trading, and grocery shopkeeping. Mahabub Hossain found that in 1987, 46% of loans went to livestock and poultry raising, 25% for processing and light manufacturing, and 23% for trading and shopkeeping; and thus almost no loans went to finance farm crop activities.

Opportunities for expansion of agricultural activities are limited in Bangladesh. About two-thirds of its 56,000 square miles is under cultivation, and the cost of expanding into the remaining uncultivated area is excessively high. Nearly three-quarters of the labor force is already working in agriculture, and opportunities for women are especially limited. Small scale "microentrepreneurship" offers the best opportunity for most of the functionally landless rural poor to improve their economic circumstances. The Grameen Bank's focus on rural women microenterprise borrowers is probably optimal, providing the highest marginal social benefits under the conditions found in rural Bangladesh.

The average loan size in 1992 was $67, about half the annual income of borrowers. Loans have generally reached the absolutely poor. Mahabub Hossain found that only 4.2% of borrowers own as much as a half acre of cultivatable land. The average income of borrowers has been found to be about half the national average. Though incomes of most borrowers remain below the poverty line, they get much closer to the line. In other words, Grameen has not much reduced poverty by the headcount measure, but has significantly reduced it by the income shortfall measure.

Grameen borrowers have had notable success in capital accumulation. Cattle raising is a major activity of borrowers. Hossain found that the number of cattle owned increased by 26% per year. Though the numbers involved are small--going from 61 per 100 borrowers before becoming a Grameen member to 102 per 100 borrowers at the time of the survey--these are impressive improvements for Bangladesh's absolutely poor.

But completely landless agricultural laborers appear to remain significantly underrepresented in the pool of borrowers: Hossain found that they represent 60% of Grameen's target group but only 20% of its actual borrowers--and this includes those who reported hired agricultural labor as a secondary as well as those who reported it a primary economic activity. These are the kinds of data that social scientists want to examine closely. There is certainly a stigma attached to being from an agricultural-labor household, and its incidence among borrowers could perhaps be understated--though likely not by much given Grameen's good information about its borrowers. In any case, to be both landless and an agricultural laborer by occupation is to be among the very most downtrodden groups in any developing country. Note that in Bangladesh, most laborers own a small plot of land for their house, but too little to form the basis for a viable farm. Some 60% of Bangladeshis are "functionally landless" in this sense.

But underreaching the hired agricultural laborers is probably not the fault of the Grameen Bank. Landless farm laborers are extremely hard to reach for any development program in any country. They also tend to be the least educated and are probably the least well prepared to move into viable entrepreneurial activities. The fact that the Bank has reached as many landless farm laborers as it has is itself very impressive. These laborers benefit indirectly from the general development that Grameen affords, as it raises demand for labor and reduces the supply of agricultural labor. They will need other services besides those the Grameen can provide. But they must be the target of renewed, concerted aid efforts.

Grameen makes some loans to finance cooperative enterprises as well as making loans to individuals. The goal is to take advantage of economies of scale and make the use of more modern techniques financially feasible. Though the share of such loans have been well under 10%, they have financed some of the most impressive undertakings, including the purchase and use of power looms, rice hullers, oil mills, and irrigation machines. But both the Bank and its borrowers have lacked the technical expertise to make these activities viable, and this is an area of needed improvement.

Grameen's emphasis on serving poor women is especially impressive. According to Hossain's survey, half the women borrowers said they were unemployed at the time they became Grameen members (compared with less than 7% of the men). The share of women among borrowers has climbed steadily over the years and has now reached 82%.

Is Grameen subsidized, and how much subsidy makes sense? Costs at the bank are quite high by commercial bank standards. They have been estimated at 26.5% of the value of loans and advances. This is some 10% higher than the nominal interest rate charged, or 39% of the costs of lending are subsidized from all sources. Adding in estimated opportunity costs, Hossain has calculated an effective subsidy of 51%.

These high cost numbers indicate at first glance that there is room for greater economy measures. But it may also indicate that interest rates charged borrowers are at least 10 percentage points too low. We have seen that these rates are only about a tenth that charged by traditional moneylenders and that repayment rates are over 97%. Most borrowers would already be better off paying an interest rate of, say 27%, since they are either paying far more already or simply have no source of borrowing at all. Only comparatively few current borrowers may be expected to find their investments no longer profitable at a higher interest rate.

However, there is no doubt that a public subsidy of Grameen loans is justifiable on the basis of their positive externalities, or spinoffs outside the market, and absolute poverty alleviation. Ideally, these benefits should be quantified to get a better handle on how much subsidy there should be. Since funds for subsidies are limited, the more the subsidy per loan, the less subsidized loans can be made. But also note that about half of the excess of costs over interest receipts are attributable to the expense of opening new branches, which should be treated as a capital cost. There may be some combination of reduced operating costs, modest increases in interest rates, and continued subsidy that is optimal for creating the most welfare gains with the available resources.

A small loans development bank like Grameen may be a vital--if not necessary--condition for improving the well-being of the poor. But it is not a sufficient condition. Bangladesh suffers many tornados and excessive floods. A terrible recent example took place in 1992, when up to 200,000 people died in flooding following a major cyclone. For the survivors, these recurrent disasters can and do also wipe out years of economic progress nurtured by Grameen. This shows that small-scale projects like Grameen are not enough and must be undertaken in conjunction with large-scale projects like Bangladesh's flood control project. The point is not that large-scale projects should be abandoned in favor of small-scale ones but that the two work together. Neither by itself is a sufficient development strategy.

The general value of the Grameen experience depends on whether it can be replicated and sustained. Its replicability has already been demonstrated in good measure both in Bangladesh and outside it. It has spread to villages in several regions of the country. Even so, it has still only covered less than 5% of its target group in Bangladesh. Only time will tell whether it can continue to expand at its previous impressive rates. Of course, while the goal of a Grameen must be to work itself out of a job, realistically millions of Bangladeshis will remain poor for several decades to come under the very best assumptions.

Though on a smaller scale, other developing countries have benefitted from imitating the Grameen Bank, including Malaysia, Sri Lanka, and Malawi. It has even been borrowed with some success as a model by some of America's inner cities, as Lewis Solomon has chronicled. Of course, it would be unrealistic to expect Grameen to be replicable everywhere. For example, training and oversight activities are very labor-intensive, and would be hard to operate efficiently with a highly dispersed population without viable roads, let alone communications. Corruption might engulf similar activities elsewhere. But although none of the existing replications have yet demonstrated that they can approach Grameen's scale and durability, their benefits to date are substantial. Grameen's own sustainability seems clear with a solid track record of over a decade.

No discussion of replicability and sustainability would be complete without noting that Grameen has greatly benefitted from the dedication of the motivated and idealistic bank staff. The Grameen Bank "organizational culture" emphasizing service to the genuinely poor has helped maintain honorable attitudes. Importantly, staff incentives are also maintained: quick promotions have been regularly awarded to those whose performance in the field has been exemplary.

A major key to Grameen's sustainability will be to keep high motivation, anti-poverty orientation, and rewards for good work intact, and to guard against the lethargy, arrogance, and corruption that mar so many other developing country bureaucracies and quasi-public financial institutions. A system of cooperatives begun among rickshaw pullers in the 1960s and once considered a model for the country lost its vitality after it was taken over by the government in the 1970s. Grameen's continued independence may be essential to its future success.

Finally, the role of a dedicated founder like Muhammad Yunus cannot be underestimated. If development aid agencies only knew better how to identify, encourage and support individuals who are motivated, technically competent, skilled at organization, charismatic, and genuinely altruistic a major step toward development progress would be made. By all accounts this is the character and achievement of Dr. Yunus, a man of great ability who could clearly have made much more money in other endeavors. Such leaders can never be fully paid for the value their good works add to society, but for some potential leaders of this calibre the prestige and renown they gain from their works might be an added incentive to pursue an altruistic career combining compassion and competence. In this case ordinary development scholars can perhaps do no better service than to publicize their achievements.

Sources. Mahmoub Hossain, "Credit for Alleviation of Rural Poverty: The Grameen Bank in Bangladesh," International Food Policy Research Institute Research Report No. 65, 1988; Christian Science Monitor, July 8, 1992; March 5, 1991; March 15, 1989; Washington Post, Feb. 14, 1993; The Economist, Oct. 18, 1986; Lewis D. Solomon, "Microenterprise: Human Reconstruction in America's Inner Cities," Harvard J. of Law and Public Policy, Winter 1992; Inderjit Singh, The Great Ascent: The Rural Poor in South Asia, Johns Hopkins, for the World Bank, 1990; S.R. Osmani, "Limits to the Alleviation of Poverty through Non-Farm Credit, The Bangladesh Development Studies, 17, 1-17, 1989.

6. Population, Famines, and Entitlement Theory: Application to the Case of Somalia

The images of famine appear and disappear from the television screens and the public awareness, just as do images of unemployment lines following the irregular fluctuations of the business cycle. We have the searing images of fly-covered children with protruding bones, bloated bellies, and sunken eyes in Biafra, Bangladesh, Ethiopia, Sudan, and recently in Somalia. Horrified by these pictures, the world springs into action and sends food. For this is how we usually think of famine: the absence of food.

The media and the public would find support for their use of the word "famine" in Webster's dictionary: "an extreme scarcity of food; a great shortage." But in Somalia, the world recently learned that simply sending food might do nothing to solve the problem. So troops were sent along with the food, and for now people have stopped starving. But is this enough? Will this approach prevent people from starving again there in the future, or prevent similar disasters from cropping up elsewhere?

In many cases, such as the terrible Bangladesh famine of 1974, famines coexist with bumper crops of food. Famines, as one might expect, may coexist with national economic declines, as with the recent Ethiopia and Somalia famines. Or, they may coexist with national economic booms, in which the incomes and purchasing power of some groups, usually nonfarmers, increase rapidly, leading them to demand more food and force up its price. This means other groups, often rural laborers whose wages do not keep pace with increases in the price of food, are left with too little income to buy the amount of food they and their children need to survive. A likely example of this was the Bengal famine of 1943. In other cases, the national scarcity of food is an effect of something else, not the prime cause of the suffering. Can development economics provide any insights to this complex problem?

This is the puzzle tackled by Amartya Sen in his celebrated 1981 theory of famines.

In Sen's terminology, the "acquirement problem" is one of "establishing command over commodities." Sen's approach to the analysis of famines disputes the focus on food availability in favor of examining changes in "endowments and exchange entitlements." Food entitlements depend on what can be grown oneself, what can be purchased with wage or other income or through the sale of assets, or finally from private charity or public welfare.

A peasant who grows his or her own food may have to sell some--or even most--of that food to meet debt or other obligations. She may suffer a food deficit if impacted by a drought or other weather shock. A laborer may lose his entitlement to food if he loses his job. Or even if she does not lose her job, a laborer may find that she has a decreased "command over" food commodities if food represents a very large share of her expenditure budget and the relative price of food rises significantly. Finally, a poor self-employed artisan, repairer or other petty service provider who offers a product or service for sale may suffer hunger if its price falls sharply relative to that of food.

In few societies is food divided equally or by need (there are certain exceptions such as some Israeli kibbutzim). And few developing countries have an effective "safety net" public assistance system. Thus those who fail to "establish command over food" may well go hungry and even starve to death. This is obvious enough, but before Sen's work all the discussion in the literature about famines and widespread starvation in developing countries focused on aggregate food availability.

Sen shows that historically, famines are more closely associated with collapses of "exchange entitlements" of specific impoverished groups of the local population than they are of declines in aggregate per capita food availability. While historians have made some of these observations in the past, this was the first analytically careful and empirically systematic work.

According to Sen's evidence, those affected by famines work in particular occupations, such as farm laborer; occupations affected differ from famine to famine and from country to country. This evidence underlines that the problem is not so much a lack of food in general, but a failure of some subgroups to exert "command" over food.

When a famine is looming it is common to find families "hoarding" food. Many will stock up on far more food than they really need, for many months in advance. In this way, the fear of famine can become a self-fulfilling prophesy, as hoarding finally creates a real shortage of food for those without it. These surges in demand for food, driven by fear, can dramatically increase its price in the short run. As a result, there can even be "bubbles" in the price of food, just as there have been in tulips, South Sea Islands shares, or Japanese stocks.

None of this means that aggregate food availability is unrelated to famines. Even with a good system of entitlements, distribution, and incentives for production, an exogenous shock such as a devastating drought or flood can be the root cause of famine. Entitlements will depend on the price of food, as we have seen, and of course a major determinant of the price of food is its aggregate availability.

The entitlements approach certainly does not mean that everyone in the developing world be simply entitled to food without expecting anything in return. Here as in designing any development program, incentives need to be kept in mind. An excellent strategy is an approach like the Food for Work Program of Bangladesh, Maharashtra State in India, and elsewhere, which guarantees on a daily basis a food allotment to anyone willing to work for it in rural infrastructure projects (the Bangladesh Food for Work Program is the subject of another case study).

Sen does not discuss expectations of future price changes and the self-fulfilling prophesy of panics over food availability and price. This is important as a dynamic that needs to be prevented, but does not affect the entitlement approach per se.

Since the early 1980s, Sen's analysis has been applied with success to a number of historical cases, as the recent volume Famines, edited by G.A. Harrison attests. But how well does it stand up to a current case, Somalia, which is perceived by many to be different from other recent famines?

Somalia.

Are the recent African famines, and the events in Somalia in particular, a challenge to Sen's theory of famines?

This is a region with the highest rates of population growth in the world. In Somalia, population growth has been 3.2% over the last 30 years, increasing the population from 2.9 to 7.5 million, according to UN statistics. All of this sounds on the surface very much like a case of a food availability shock if not the beginnings of a Malthusian collapse.

In the period leading up to the Somalia famine, aggregate food production did decline, some 21% from the mid-seventies to the mid-eighties according to calculations by Dreze and Sen using Food and Agriculture Organization (FAO) data.

Somalia's economy was fragile and inefficient for many years. The corrupt regime of longtime dictator Mohammed Siad Barre was a severe restraint on development in the country. But the proximate cause of the civic and economic collapse of Somalia was Barre's ouster in early 1991. In the capital area, rival local and migrant clans and organized crime bands struggled for political control and embezzled wealth with increasing violence.

The country went from inefficient and corrupt government to essentially no government (excepting private violence for private gain), so that not even the rudiments of the right to personal safety or basic property rights were available. Under such circumstances there is little incentive to produce anything. Certainly there was a dramatic decrease in the availability of Somalia-produced food--but this was the proximate, not the root cause of the famine.

At the height of the famine in late 1992, thousands of people were dying daily and millions were at risk of imminent starvation. Under weakened conditions of undernutrition, people, especially small children, become much more susceptible to disease. The immediate cause of death for many was dehydration caused by diarrhea, and bacterial infections, especially pneumonia.

We still have no reliable estimates of the number of deaths in Somalia; one effect of the evaporation of central government was the cessation of any collection of health statistics beginning in early 1991. But preliminary indications are that Somalia will represent one of the deadliest famines in recorded history. Upwards of 300,000 Somalis are estimated to have starved to death or died of complications of starvation in 1992. About 30,000 died in the accompanying violence.

A report by the Atlanta-based Center for Disease Control on two Somali towns it surveyed in late 1992 concluded that mortality rates were among "the highest ever documented in a population survey among famine-infected civilians." More than half of the population of 30,000 in the town of Baidoa, one of the warlord strongholds, is estimated to have died, including 70% of children under age five, between April and November 1992. The report concluded that conditions were substantially worse than during the peak mortality periods of the Ethiopian famine of 1984-85.

Somalia showed that Sen's term, "command over commodities," was no hyperbole. When the economy is collapsing and people have no entitlements, control of food means power over hungry people, plain and simple. What went on in Somalia under the invading warlords does not remotely represent the "magic of the marketplace," nor did the exchange that went on between warlords and terrified people resemble anything like a free market exchange.

In some ways the case of Somalia is as direct an example of Sen's theory as could be found in recent history. A member of a warlord's gang or favored circle has command over food, and others do not.

In the case of Somalia, the government had in 1987 formulated a basic minimum needs program based on community participation and integrated rural development modeled on the program in Thailand, one of the first of its kind. By 1991 it had been implemented in 36 villages with about 20,000 people. International organizations such as the World Health Organization were deeply involved. Significant progress in areas such as immunizations, safe drinking water, reduction of malnutrition, and primary school attendance were recorded within a year of the program's operation.

The program was small in relation to Somalia's population of 7.5 million people. Government was corrupt in the large even if small parts of it were honest and dedicated. It is very unclear that the program could have been successfully expanded even without the collapse of its government.

Although the program was interrupted by the collapse of central governmental authority in Somalia, the small program did show that an entitlements approach to famine aversion and development is possible in Somalia. The causes of its problems are internal, socio-economic ones, not the caprices of rainfall and climate. While drought afflicts Somalia as it does many other countries in the region, the permanent solution to its problems are not food aid nor necessarily even increased food production but to establish sustainable "command over commodities" for the poorest of the poor. The influx of food into Somalia caused the market price of food to drop significantly. Price elasticities have not been estimated but it is feared that local production will be substantially affected.

More important is what goes on at the local level. The image of ruthless anarchy occurring throughout the country is something of an exaggeration of the reality. This characterized the southwest region near the capital, and the region around two other cities. But in other parts of the country, traditional governance of elders reasserted itself and provided for a relatively peaceful society, one producing at least the minimum basic needs for most of the people.

Sen's "exchange entitlement" approach can be applied to the problem of effective famine anticipation and action. Shifts in food entitlement are the best early warning system that famine may be in the cards. Policies that address entitlement needs rather than just aggregate food supply are likely to represent the most effective anti-famine strategies.

The contrast between Somalia and some other African countries, such as

Zimbabwe and Botswana, as well as some other low-income countries such as India, is striking. We will look a little more closely at the case of Zimbabwe (Botswana is touched on in the case study on Zaire). A long period of racial conflict came to an end in Zimbabwe when democracy was established there in 1980. Robert Mugabe's Zimbabwe African National Union made social services, especially in health, nutrition and education, its top priority; and it began to make immediate progress.

But the government was quickly tested by a severe three-year drought lasting from 1982 to 1984. The drought caused a collapse in the production of corn, Zimbabwe's staple crop. Coupled with the still highly dualistic distribution of farmland, starvation was a very real possibility for many Zimbabweans. But the government acted quickly, initiating substantial food distribution measures for the adult population and targeted supplementary feeding programs for children under 5 years of age. Studies vary in their estimates of how many people benefitted, but are unanimous in their conclusion that food got to the many who needed it in sufficient quantities to prevent starvation and even improve the health status of the poor in this period.

Dreze and Sen conclude, along with many other foreign academic and journalist observers, that an important factor in Zimbabwe's success was its free society, notably its no-holds-barred press, grass-roots political participation and active political debate.

Dreze and Sen note that other countries which have earned high marks for avoiding threatened famines, such as Botswana and India, are also stable democracies, at least by Third World standards.

This finding that democracy matters for the alleviation of poverty is the basic needs justification for making progress toward democracy a precondition for all but emergency aid, a trend in most aid agencies. The principle of non-interference in internal affairs in the face of undemocratic and corrupt regimes is an idea whose time has passed when it comes to the provision of foreign aid.

Sen's theory of famines is better at explaining the terrible recent events of Somalia than traditional ideas based on the availability of food. War and civic collapse are one more way that peoples' entitlements to food may be taken away. As Sen has noted, the frequent association of famine with war is not just the result of the destruction of productive capacity that war brings, or the diversion of resources to military uses, or even the disruption of social services and relief operations. Conditions such as we have seen in Somalia also greatly reduce the incentive to produce food, and local aggregate food availability may fall. But the democracy link is also strong. War provides the excuse and the method for suppressing freedom of the press and other democratic institutions. This in turn blocks the channel for popular outcry that could rally public resources for food entitlements.

As relief grain piled up on Somali docks while thousands died daily, it became clear that famines are not caused by the unavailability of food, but by lack of entitlements to it by the afflicted segments of society.

Sources. Barzgar, M.A., and I.A. Kore, "A Solid Base for Health," World Health Forum, 12, 156-169, 1991; Said S. Samatar, "How to Save Somalia," Washington Post, Nov. 25, Dec. 1, and Dec. 27, 1992; Jan. 9, Jan. 16, Jan. 30 and Feb. 6, 1993; New York Times, Jan. 19, 1993; Sen, Amartya Kumar, Poverty and famines : an essay on entitlement and deprivation, New York : Oxford University Press, 1981; Sen, Amartya Kumar, "Peacekeeping and Starvation: On the Somalian and Other Crises in Sub-Saharan Africa," Paper presented at the AEA Annual Meetings, Anaheim, Jan. 1993; Jean Dreze and Amartya Kumar Sen, Hunger and Public Action, New York : Oxford University Press, 1989; Martin Ravallion, Markets and Famines, Oxford: Clarendon, 1987; Harrison, G.A., ed., Famines, New York : Oxford University Press, 1988; UNDP, Human Development Report, 1992.

7. The Choice of Appropriate Technology: A World Bank Study of Textiles in Kenya and the Philippines

There has been a large debate over the choice of an "appropriate technology" for developing countries. But the debate has been very abstract, and it often seems to professionals concerned with development that little useful progress has been made in the real world. But a recent World Bank study conducted by Professor Howard Pack of the University of Pennsylvania has pointed the way to making real progress on this problem.

The basic dilemma facing developing countries is that while they generally have abundant labor and scarce capital, innovations are usually made in advanced countries which generally have abundant capital and scarce labor. If a developing country wants to use a more labor-intensive technique, this generally means using an older technique, and so generally a less productive one. Technology progress is made in the use of capital as well as labor, though labor-saving techniques are often much more visible. (With the drastic price decreases of computers even as their power rapidly expands, consider how much less capital it takes to perform a given computer calculation today as compared with just ten years ago).

In the extreme, some writers have said that there could be a conflict between output and employment. Using a labor-intensive technique might involve using a technology so backward that the limited capital involved was utilized so inefficiently, that an increase in the number of workers might entail a decrease in the level of output.

That the output-employment tradeoff is possible can be seen from this example. Suppose traditional looms cost 1000 rupees each, with 100 laborers employed at one loom per worker. The modern technique saves not only labor but capital: the same output is now produced by 25 workers in a shop with 50,000 rather than 100,000 rupees of capital equipment. Of course, one can always use modern equipment and pay surplus workers to do nothing--but this is hardly a recipe for international competitiveness. But these arguments generally come from rather casual observation of particular examples. What has been lacking is a systematic and careful study.

This makes it seem that developing countries have limited range to take advantage of their abundant labor in international trade. The United Nations and other development agencies have increasingly attempted in recent years to innovate technology for developing countries that is at once labor-intensive and scientifically and technologically modern. Some progress has been made in areas like small scale pumping and irrigation technology. But the private sector, where resources for applied technical innovation are concentrated, has been little involved and the rate of progress has been rather disappointing.

If innovating technology for developing countries that is labor-intensive and technologically modern would lead to significant gains in efficiency, why has the private sector been so little involved? Or does this mean that appropriate technology is less valuable than development economists have maintained? The problem seems to be not so much that appropriate technology is unprofitable but that the profits cannot easily be appropriated by the innovator. Developing countries where appropriate technology might be used tend to lack intellectual property rights that would provide the innovator a return on investment in creating the technology. The problem of information and opportunism is equally important, and this is especially true for more basic types of technology. By the time the inventor explains enough about the invention to the potential licensee to convince her of the value of the technique, he may already have had to tell her enough about how it works for her to be able to carry on independently. Each of these factors obviously decreases the incentive for private firms to engage in this type of innovation.

At the same time, it remains the case that the use of higher technology production equipment in developing countries has been for the most part disappointing. While there are exceptions such as South Korean conglomerates and some "Maquiladora" factories operated by U.S. multinational corporations just below the border in Mexico, for the most part the use of advanced technology in developing countries has not produced the payoffs claimed by its producers or users in developed countries.

Numerous studies have shown that in many sectors, there is more room for substitution of labor for capital than meets the eye. Simple strategies like having extra shifts so that machines are never shut down, specialized personnel to maintain equipment at peak performance at all times, and so on can increase output while decreasing the effective capital-labor ratio. Moreover, older--but not antiquated--technologies do sometimes dominate the most advanced ones at developing country factor prices such as wages of unskilled workers.

The distinguishing characteristic of industry in the developing world is its low productivity. There are market failures in the transfer of technology from developed to developing countries. That such market failures are endemic to original technological progress is one of the best known propositions in economics. But there are also market failures in the transfer of product, process and organizational innovations to developing countries. Many developing countries have conducted an active "infant" industrial strategy, designed to protect local industries long enough for them to reach efficient production levels. But the validity of these policies depends in part on the ability of infants to really increase their productivity over time.

As Pack notes, higher-tech equipment that is projected to be more efficient (in unit production costs) when evaluated using a developing country's lower wages but developed countries' productivity specifications may prove less efficient than more conventional equipment when evaluated at developing countries' lower productivity norms--which tend to hold even after the infant has grown up.

In other words, we must consider realistic production requirements (input coefficients) for a specific country rather than general manufacturers' specifications. With cheaper labor, developing countries do not have to reach the same productivity standards as developed countries, but they cannot have productivity standards that are proportionally even lower than their wages. Thus issues of productivity and the choice of an appropriate technology are closely interconnected.

To address these important issues directly, Pack's study compared companies using identical equipment in Kenya and the Philippines with those in developed countries, primarily in the United Kingdom. The study required Prof. Pack, an economist, to venture well beyond the usual range for economic analysis. Rather than take technical specifications as a given provided by engineers, he had to study them directly. In doing so, he had to learn technical details of spinning and weaving technology. But crossing disciplinary boundaries in this way is often the source of real intellectual progress.

Prof. Pack analyzed production data from a large number of individual plants in Kenya and the Philippines, and compared their productivity with "best-practice plants" in England. Best practice rather than engineering coefficients is relevant because human factors are crucial in the actual efficiency of a manufacturing plant in a way that engineering specifications simply cannot capture. Total factor productivity (TFP) comparisons were made, which measures difference in output performance once standard inputs like capital and labor have been accounted for. These analyses confirmed that total factor productivity tended to fall well short of best practice norms in both Kenya and the Philippines.

In spinning, plants in both countries achieved about 70% of the total factor productivity as found in plants using the same equipment the United Kingdom. In weaving, only about 55% of total factor productivity was found in the Philippines, and 68% in Kenya, relative to the United Kingdom. Sources of these differences include inefficiencies in the national economy, in the organization of the plant and other management responsibilities, and in the performance of individual workers. But an important problem was the failure to achieve economies of product specialization, such as can found in Italy. As Prof. Pack demonstrates, the international evidence suggests that a liberal trade regime is a necessary but not a sufficient condition to ensure that product specialization economies are realized. Increasing competitive pressure on firms must be only one component of industrial upgrading policy.

Prof. Pack's conclusions were both very concrete and specific for the textile industry, and offered general principles to look for in evaluations of other industries. Neither the most modern nor the most traditional technology provided the best practice in the Philippines or Kenya. Most cost-efficient technologies in these countries tended to be intermediate in sophistication. Employing used intermediate-vintage equipment rather than new intermediate equipment was also shown to be cost-saving in many cases; there is a tendency for it to be used more effectively relative to its best-use potential, and it can often be bought at good prices. As the case of Philippine weaving showed, astute management decisions regarding the amount of labor to use with such equipment can result in large cost savings.

A wide range of evidence from engineering data to interviews led to the conclusion that the mastery of a new technology is not simply the result of the proverbial "learning by doing." Mastery takes more than experience, but requires targeted expenditures and considered management.

Inappropriate technology is caused by other factors besides underpriced capital and overpriced urban modern sector labor. The available information is often poor; managers may think their selection of high technology will sound better on the golf course, and technology is probably not always as flexible as Prof. Pack found it to be in the textile industry. But factor pricing policy-- removing subsidies for capital use and eliminating large artificial wage premiums for work in the modern sector--has an important role to play.

Appropriate technology availability problems are real. But Professor Pack's important study has demonstrated that there is room for developing countries to manoeuver, and shown a strategy for evaluating best available options.

Sources. Howard Pack, Productivity, Technology and Industrial Development, New York: Oxford Univ. Press for the World Bank, 1987; Chenery, Nollis, Sherwin Robinson, and Moses Syrquin, 1986, Industrialization and Growth: A comparative study, New York: Oxford; Carl J. Dahlman, Bruce Ross-Larson and Larry E. Westphal, "Managing Technical Development: Lessons from the Newly Industrializing Countries," World Development, 15, 759-75, 1987; Howard Pack and Larry Westphal, "Industrial Strategy and Technological Change: Theory versus Reality," Journal of Development Economics, 22, 87-128, 1986; Stephen C. Smith, Industrial Policy in Developing Countries: Reconsidering the Real Sources of Export Led Growth, Economic Policy Institute, 1991.

8. Rural Migration and Urbanization in Developing Countries: The Cases of India and Botswana

Urban population growth in the developing world is far more rapid than population growth generally; about half the urban growth is accounted for by migrants from the rural areas. Third World cities are growing far more rapidly than those in the First World. What drives migration? What effects does this have? The cases of India and Botswana are instructive in showing the value of the development theory of migration, as well as some areas where it needs to be extended.

As Dipak Mazumdar has demonstrated, relative rates of urbanization are not higher in developing countries today than they were in the period of rapid urbanization of today's developed countries. But in today's developing countries this migration is different for at least two important reasons: it is much higher in terms of absolute numbers of migrants; and in recent years it has been taking place in many cases against a background of stagnant living standards rather than one of growth. Problems caused by urbanization like stress on infrastructure and other urban services are likely greater.

Shantytowns and similar makeshift settlements represent over one-third of Third World urban residences. Unchecked urbanization of the developing world is placing a strain on infrastructure and public health and threatens social stability.

About half of the urban labor force works in the informal sector of low-skilled, low-productivity, often self-employed jobs in petty sales and services. Still, this sector may generate up to a third of urban income, and features a low capital intensity, low cost training, waste recycling, and creation of surplus as well as employment creation.

Any economic or social policy that affects rural and urban incomes will influence migration; this in turn will affect sectoral and geographic economic activity, income distribution and even population growth. Before the Todaro migration models were introduced, migration was widely viewed as irrational or driven by noneconomic motivations sometimes termed the "bright city lights." Noneconomic factors influence migration decisions, but economic factors are primary.

In the economic version of the bright city lights theory, people rationally migrated on the basis of costs and benefits. In this approach, it was assumed that if migrants appeared to be worse off, this was because other benefits were being overlooked, that had the effect of making the migrants feel better off (or raised their overall utility).

The Todaro migration models postulate that observed migration is individually rational and that migrants respond to urban-rural differences in expected rather than actual earnings. Urban modern sector earnings are much higher than rural earnings, which may in turn be even higher than urban traditional sector earnings. Migration occurs until average, or expected rather than actual incomes are equal across regions, generating equilibrium urban unemployment or underemployment in the traditional sector.

The extension of the model to consider equilibrium and effects of actions like increases in wages and probability of employment in the urban areas, undertaken by Harris and Todaro, shows that under some conditions, notably elastic supply of labor, creation of employment opportunities in cities can actually lead to an increase in unemployment.

Despite being individually rational, extensive rural-urban migration produces social costs including lowered output and stress on infrastructure. Relevant migration and employment policies include an emphasis on rural development, rural basic needs strategies, elimination of factor price distortions, and appropriate technology choice as well as appropriate education.

Excessive migration also imposes external costs on the rural areas emptied of better-educated, more venturesome young people as well as external costs on urban infrastructure and lost output.

Migrants tend to be younger and better educated than non-migrants, and come from all socio-economic strata. Almost by definition they seem to show above-average entrepreneurial drive. Thus, paradoxically, migrants seem to have slightly better prospects in the rural areas than those who do not migrate.

India provides an interesting setting for a case study, because future urban migration is potentially so vast, and because a number of interesting studies have been undertaken there. Botswana offers a good counterpoint, because it has better published data and more advanced statistical analysis of that data has been undertaken there.

One of the best detailed studies of the economics of rural-urban migration, providing some tests of the Todaro migration models and depicting the characteristics of migrants and the migration process, is Biswajit Banerjee's Rural to Urban Migration and the Urban Labor Market: A Case Study of Delhi.

Everyone who has been to a major city in a developing country has noticed the sharp inequality between those with modern sector jobs and those scratching out a living in the informal sector. But can the informal sector be seen as a waystation to the formal sector, or can the barriers be explained by education and skill levels? Banerjee found that the idea of segmented formal-informal rural labor markets could be substantiated statistically. After carefully controlling for human capital variables, Banerjee was still left with earnings in the formal sector 9% higher than in the informal sector that were not explained by any standard economic factor.

We should not automatically assume that when we observe those with more schooling receiving higher earnings that this is a direct reflection of more skills learned in school. It may be that employers simply hire more educated workers as a way of selecting among their many job applicants. It should be noted that there are differences in wages across industries even in a developed country such as the United States. Even so, the earnings differences were not nearly so dramatic as implied in some of the migration literature. Interestingly, wage discrimination was found among members of lower ("scheduled") castes in the formal sector, but not in the informal sector. This may reflect the failure of India's affirmative action policies to permeate the unregulated informal sector effectively.

In the literature on urbanization, and in the anecdotes told about the informal sector by lecturers on development the world over (including the present author), the typical laborer is characterized as self-employed or working on some type of piecework basis. But Banerjee found that only some 14% of his informal sector sample worked in nonwage employment. Interestingly, average monthly income of nonwage workers were some 47% higher than those of formal sector workers.

Banerjee argued that entry into nonwage employment was not easy in Delhi. Some activities required significant skills or capital. Those that did not were often controlled by cohesive "networks" of operators which controlled location of activities in various enterprises. Entry barriers to self-employment in petty services are probably lower in other Third World cities.

Consistent with these findings, Banerjee found that mobility from the informal to the formal sector was low: there was little evidence that more than a very small minority of informal sector workers were actively seeking jobs in the formal sectors; and only 5 to 15% of rural migrants into the informal sector had moved over to the formal sector within a year.

Moreover, the rate of entrants into the formal sector from the informal sector was just one-sixth to one-third that of the rate of direct entry to the urban formal sector from outside the area. Informal sector workers tended to work in the same job almost as long as those in the formal sector: the average informal sector worker had worked 1.67 jobs over a period of 61 months in the city, while formal sector workers averaged 1.24 jobs over an urban career of 67 months.

Banerjee's survey data suggested that a large number of informal sector workers had migrated to the city attracted by the informal rather than the formal sector, coming to work in such occupations as domestic servants, informal construction laborers and sales workers. Of those who began nonwage employment upon their arrival, 71% had expected to do so. The fact that only a minority of informal sector workers continued to search for formal sector work was taken as further evidence that migrants had come to Delhi expressly to take up informal sector work.

One reason for this focus on the informal sector was concluded to be the lack of contacts of informal sector workers in the formal sector. About two thirds of direct entrants into the formal sector and some 60% of those switching from the informal to the formal sector found their jobs through "contacts." This overwhelming importance of contacts was taken to explain why some 43% of Banerjee's sample migrated after receiving a suggestion from a contact, which suggests that job market information is often available to potential migrants without their being physically present in the city. An additional 10% of the sample had a prearranged job in the city prior to migration.

Finally, there is on average a very short spell of unemployment following migration: 64% had found employment within one week, and although a few were unemployed for a long period, even averaging these in, the average waiting time to obtain a first job was just 17 days.

Banerjee also found that migrants kept close ties to their rural roots. Some three-quarters of the migrants visited their villages of origin and about two-thirds were remitting part of their urban incomes, a substantial 23% on average. This indicates that concern for the whole family appeared to be a guiding force in migration. It also points up the rapid flow of job market information from urban to rural areas.

In a separate study, A.S. Oberai, Pradhan Prasad, and M.G. Sardana examined the determinants of migration in three states in India: Bihar, Kerala, and Uttar Pradesh. Their findings were very much consistent with the idea that migrants often have a history of chronic unemployment before they migrate, migrate only as a measure of desperation, and with the intention of participating in the informal urban sector even in the long run. Remittances were found to be substantial and considerable levels of return-migration were also documented, among other evidence of continued close ties of migrants to their home villages.

Of course, Delhi in particular and India in general may be different from other developing areas. As a whole, these two studies have been taken as a challenge to the applicability of Harris-Todaro or other "probabilistic migration models" at least in the case of India and suggest that they need to be extended to accommodate the apparently common pattern of migrating with the ultimate aim of urban informal sector employment..

But Banerjee's findings, fascinating as they are, do not necessarily represent as strong a case against the Todaro migration models as some (including Banerjee) have made them out to be. As Ira Gang has noted, one can modify the model to include in the urban area not only a formal sector, but a high paid informal sector, as well as a low paid (or unemployed) sector. In this case, people will migrate looking for either a Formal sector job or a High Paid Informal sector job. This seems to be consistent with Banerjee's evidence. The assumption that keeps the essence of the Todaro models intact is that the wage of the formal urban sector exceeds the high-paid informal wage, which in turn exceeds the agricultural wage, and in turn exceeds the low paid informal (or unemployed) wage. The particular formulations of the Todaro models are really no more than examples of a general principle, that migrants go where they expect in advance to do better, not where they do better after the fact. The essence of the ideas of the Todaro models do not depend on a particular idea of an informal or a formal sector.

Oded Stark's ideas on a family's use of migration can be a useful supplement to the Todaro models, and may apply to some of Banerjee's findings. In this view, a family will send members to different areas as a "portfolio diversification" strategy, to reduce the risk that the family will have no income. This approach is useful to explain any observed migration from higher to lower wage areas, and into higher wage areas, but not necessarily the area with the highest expected wage. The basic idea of the Todaro models still applies, but this approach looks at families rather than individuals, and stresses risk aversion.

In other studies, the Todaro migration models have held up well without modification in other parts of the world. The survey by Dipak Mazumdar showed that the evidence is overwhelming that migration decisions are made according to rational economic motivations. But most of these have used macro-level data not really designed to address the Todaro hypotheses directly.

A recent study of migration behavior conducted by Robert E. B. Lucas in Botswana addressed such problems in the most economically and statistically sophisticated empirical study of migration in a developing country. His econometric model consisted of four groups of equations: for employment, earnings, internal migration, and migration to South Africa; and each group was estimated from microeconomic data on individual migrants and nonmigrants. Very detailed demographic information was available in the survey used.

Rural migrants in Botswana move to five modest urban centers (they would be called towns rather than cities in many parts of the world) as well as to neighboring South Africa. Lucas found that unadjusted urban earnings are much higher than rural earnings--68% higher for males--but these differences become much smaller when schooling and experience are controlled for.

Lucas' careful estimations confirm that the higher a person's expected earnings and the higher the estimated probability of employment given a move to an urban center, the greater the chances that they will migrate. And the higher the estimated wage and probability of employment for a person in their home village, the lower the chances that they will migrate. This result was very "robust"--not sensitive to which subgroups were examined or the way various factors were controlled for--and statistically significant. It represents clear evidence in support of Todaro's original hypothesis.

Moreover, Lucas estimated that at current pay differentials, the creation of one job in an urban center would draw more than one new migrant from the rural areas, thus confirming the Harris-Todaro effect. Earnings were also found to rise significantly the longer a migrant had been in an urban center, holding education and age constant. But the reason was increases in the rate of pay rather than in the probability of employment.

Taken together, the best-conducted studies of urbanization confirm the value of the Todaro migration models as the best place to start in seeking explanations of rural to urban migration in developing countries. But these studies underscore the need to expand these explanations of migration to accommodate the fact that many today migrate to participate in the informal rather than the formal urban sector.

This may be one factor keeping modern sector wages well above informal sector wages for indefinite periods of time despite high measured urban underemployment. Workers who appear underemployed may not consider themselves as such, may perceive no possibility of moving into the modern sector, may be unable to effectively search for modern sector work while busy employed in the informal sector, and so do not create as much downward pressure on modern sector wages as it would first appear.

Sources: Michael P. Todaro, "A Model of Labor Migration and Urban Unemployment in LDCs," American Economic Review 59, 1, 138-48 (1969) and John Harris, and Michael P. Todaro, "Migration, Unemployment and Development: A Two-Sector Analysis, American Economic Review 60, 126-42 (1970); Corden, W.M. and Findlay, R., "Urban Unemployment, Intersectoral Capital Mobility and Development Policy, Economica, 42, 37-78, 1975; Cole, William E. and Sanders, Richard D., "Internal migration and urban employment in the Third World," American Economic Review 75 (June '85) p. 481-94; Lucas, Robert E. B. Emigration to South Africa's mines. American Economic Review 77 (June '87) p. 313-30; Lucas, Robert E. B. Migration amongst the Batswana. Economic Journal 95 (June '85) p. 358-82; Banerjee, Biswajit, Rural to Urban Migration and the Urban Labor Market: A Case Study of Delhi, Bombay: Himalaya Publishing House, 1986; Banerjee, Biswajit, "The role of the informal sector in the migration process: a test of probabilistic migration models and labour market segmentation for India," Oxford Economic Papers 35 1983 p. 399-422; A.S. Oberai, Pradhan Prasad, and M.G. Sardana, Determinants and Consequences of Internal Migration in India: Studies in Bihar, Kerala and Uttar Pradesh, Delhi: Oxford (1989); Dipak Mazumdar, "Rural-urban migration in Developing Countries," Handbook of Regional and Urban Economics, Vol. 2, Elsevier, 1987; Oded Stark, The migration of labor, Cambridge, MA: B. Blackwell, 1991; Ira N. Gang and Shubhashis Gangopadhyay, "A Model of the Informal sector in development, Journal of Economic Studies, vol 17, 1990 pp 19-31.

9. Agricultural Extension for Women: The Case of Kenya

The crucial importance of a solid agricultural extension program for successful rural development has been appreciated by development specialists for decades. Support for agricultural extension has played a central role in the activities of most multilateral and bilateral development agencies. Historically, agricultural extension programs played a vital development role in the United States, one of the world's great agricultural productivity success stories.

That is the good news. The bad news is that extension in developing countries has been aimed almost exclusively at training men, but women do most of the agricultural work. In Sub-Saharan Africa, women generate some 70% of staple foods production. They are also active in growing and marketing cash crops, in food processing, and animal husbandry.

In part, the prominent role of women in agriculture reflects long tradition; but women's roles have expanded in recent years as men have increasingly migrated to urban areas and taken on other nonagricultural tasks. Where men and women both do agricultural work, there still tends to be a gender-based division of labor. As a result, techniques relevant to the work of men are often not relevant to the work of women. Where they are relevant, for various reasons men tend not to pass on what they have learned to their wives (what has been called "trickle across").

The role of women in agriculture has been widely publicized in development circles in recent years. The first breakthrough was Ester Bosrup's 1970 book, <u>Women's Role in Economic Development</u>. Her work began a trend of important research in this area and a slowly dawning realization on the part of the profession that the issue of women in agriculture was at the very core of prospects for genuine development--and not a narrow concern of a faction of feminists, as some perceived it at first.

Moreover, the focus on training men has generally been more by default than by deliberate design. For example, training is copied from developed countries like the United States, where men do the majority of agricultural work; and in LDCs male extension agents may simply be more comfortable talking to men. But the agricultural extension program response to the problem has been all too slow. And in some countries, program design reflects explicit bias against providing women with too much independence.

A major problem is the segregation and exclusion of women in large parts of

Africa and Asia. Gender relations in rural areas are characterized by extreme inequality. In many cases this is a symptom of backwardness and an unacceptable violation of human rights. But one does not have to be an ardent cultural relativist to recognize that the development specialist usually can have little impact on culture.

In the present period, before progress on women's rights can be made, development specialists will have to learn to work around such practices. One emerging strategy is to make use of radio and television; and audio and, increasingly, even video tapes. Women may listen to or watch the materials in groups in houses or at village centers. Katrin Saito reports that female farmers question extension agents in Ghana about subjects they have heard discussed on the radio.

A recent World Bank study showed that most male African extension agents perceived women as "wives of farmers," rather than as farmers in their own right. And almost all extension agents are themselves male. Female agents must be trained. This is only one reason why education of rural girls is a key in development.

Agricultural extension for women is interconnected with a number of other important rural development and women in development issues. Five key ones are:

1. Human capital. Women have far less education than men on average in most rural developing areas. The bias in agricultural extension has exacerbated this relative deficiency.

2. Appropriate technology. The fact that women tend to be involved in different farm activities from men means that they will often have different technology requirements. Most technology development has been focused on activities of men.

3. Land reform and agrarian design. On average, women farm on much smaller, more fragmented plots than men; are less likely to have secure ownership; and often cultivate less fertile soil. This distribution is likely to be inefficient as well as distributionally inequitable.

4. Credit. Women have less access, if any, to financial credit, a key input in efficient agriculture.

5. Work requirements. Many women who work as many hours per day as men in agricultural pursuits also have to perform several hours of domestic work that does not apply to men. Working days for poor women farmers in Africa have been estimated at

16 to 19 hours. The attention mothers can give to children will be limited by long agricultural hours. The implication may be that women should receive an even higher priority for technical education and technology development and access. Duncan Thomas reports evidence that fathers allocate resources disproportionately toward sons and mothers toward daughters in countries as disparate as the United States, Brazil and Ghana. The priority of womens' agricultural productivity goes hand in hand with the priority of educating girls.

The latter point has particular relevance to the design of structural adjustment programs. As Rekha Mehra has noted, one intent of structural adjustment programs in many African countries is to encourage the shift to exportable cash crops. But these are the crops over which men tend to have control. A woman's share after working with these crops may be as little as one part in twenty. But she is still responsible for growing consumption crops and feeding her children. Mehra concludes that structural adjustment programs tend to place even more time requirements on women already burdened with 16 hour days and longer.

An International Food Policy Research Institute (IFPRI) study showed that after diversification to commercial crops, Kenyan women still try to grow the same amount of consumption crops. More than price adjustments are needed; reform must address structural problems faced by women that will prevent them from responding to price signals efficiently. But as David Sahn and Lawrence Haddad have stressed, blame cannot be placed primarily on structural adjustment programs for the predicament of women farmers in Africa today; conditions for women were abysmal prior to reform.

None of these problems are limited to Africa. For example, Carmen Deere, in a review of 13 Latin American agrarian reform experiences, found that most have directly benefitted only men. This was mostly because farmers were thought of as men and the reforms were designed to target only men as beneficiaries. Her review found that women only benefit in the rare instances when their wellbeing is a specific objective of the reform and rural women are made an explicit part of the design of programs from the outset.

In sum, taken as a whole these points show why women farmers need the help of extension programs. It is also efficient to do this because of an application of the law of diminishing returns to training for men; and because the theory of "trickle across"--that trained husbands will in turn train their wives--rarely occurs in practice in Africa.

At last, progress is being made, and Kenya is a good example both of successful improvements made and of the work that remains to be accomplished. The Ministry of Agriculture operates a National Extension System (NES) in concert with its agricultural research efforts.

Before 1983, the NES worked almost exclusively with male farmers, while a separate "home economics branch" advised women on household and cottage industry management, and domestic hygiene, but only peripherally on farming matters. Research by the Institute of Development Studies in Nairobi, and other agencies, confirmed that extension was much more likely to have reached men than women farmers. In 1983, Kenya's present training and visit (T&V) system was established with the express purpose of training women as well as men in efficient agricultural practices. The design of the T&V system is extremely creative.

The T&V system is based around providing "technical messages" to selected "contact farmers," who are regularly visited on their farmsteads. Unfortunately, there are not resources to reach all farmers, or if the T&V system did try to reach all farmers the quality of training would be poor. As a result, only 10% of all farmers are chosen as "contact farmers." These selected participants are expected not only to adopt advice brought to them in these "messages," but to help spread this new technical knowledge by persuading other farmers in the villages to adopt them as well. A number of "follower farmers" are expected to attend meetings with T&V officials on the contact farmer's farmstead. In this way, technical "diffusion" is maximized in a cost-effective manner.

Obviously, the selection process is vital. Farmers must be selected who are capable, likely to diligently follow through on new information, and to be locally respected so as to encourage emulation. In choosing "contact farmers," T&V officials meet with farmers and generally consult with local communities and their leaders.

At first, messages focus on procedures that do not require any cash expenditure, such as spacing and pruning. The messages being diffused in any one month are linked to farm activities underway in the annual crop cycle, such as planting or harvesting whichever crops are cultivated at a given point in the course of the year. Only as farmers see results from this initial advice and so come to trust the T&V "messages," are measures requiring modest cash outlays introduced, such as fertilizer use and crop spraying. In a later stage, measures requiring purchase of capital goods may be introduced.

Recent Kenyan and World Bank studies confirm that while not all women are yet being reached by extension services, significant progress has been made. Increasing numbers of women function officially as "contact farmers." Even more serve unofficially in this role, as their husbands farm only part-time or not at all.

The messages of the T&V program, at least ideally, are supposed to be transmitted in both directions. T&V agents are supposed to gather information about how well previous advice has worked in practice, and about continued problems, in order to guide research efforts. This is in the spirit of the often touted but seldom fulfilled "participation in development" ideal.

Economic advancement of women farmers is also important for promoting environmentally sustainable development. In addition to their responsibility for agriculture, especially on more marginal and often ecologically fragile lands, women have a customary role in traditional societies as the 'guardians of natural resources,' such as the water supply. This is also an important domain for agricultural extension work with women. In Kenya the T&V system is not yet strongly involved in environmental problems.

But thousands of women are taking part in the Green Belt Movement (GBM), established in 1977 by the National Council of Women. Its main objective, as reported by Wangari Maathai, is to "halt desertification by encouraging tree planting and soil and water conservation in rural communities." It also works to promote sustainable development and poverty alleviation in parallel projects. While initiated and run privately, seedlings are provided by the government at low prices, and GBM volunteers receive advice and support from government forestry officials, a type of extension service.

The GBM emphasizes grass-roots participation and self-help, and strives to educate people on the link between deforestation, erosion, poor soil quality and subsequent low crop yields. With the help of outside funding, women are paid to work at about one thousand nurseries. Seedlings grown at these nurseries are given to small farmers, schools and churches, which have planted an estimated 10 million surviving trees. The estimated survival rate is 70-80%. The GBM is now striving to disseminate its model throughout Africa.

The T&V system has also made less progress in the field of women's credit, and private voluntary organizations have not been there to take up the slack. A 1982 study by Kathleen Staudt found that of eighty-four female farm managers interviewed in the Kakamega District in Western Province, only one knew about the credit program, and no female manager had received any credit. Informal indications are that this is the area that has improved least over the subsequent decade.

As Christina Gladwin and Della McMillan have argued, much more must be done; for example women should be consulted at the design stage of technology development, extension specialists should receive training on how to approach a male farmer about training his wife or wives; and governments should target funds to women's organizations and clubs.

Training and provision of credit and other inputs for women farmers is one of the critical areas where development professionals can have the biggest impact on reducing poverty, and inequality, and fostering genuine development.

Sources. Katrin Saito and C. Jean Weidemann, "Agricultural Extension for Women Farmers in Sub-Saharan Africa," World Bank Discussion Paper No. 103, 1990; Katrin Saito, Extending Help to Women Farmers in LDCs," Finance and Development, Sept. 1991; Ester Bosrup, Women's Role in Economic Development, New York: St. Martin's Press, 1970; Duncan Thomas, Gender Differences in Household Resource Allocations, World Bank Living Standards Measurement Study Paper 79; Jean Davison, ed., "Agriculture, Women and Land: The African Experience," London: Westview Press, Kenya: The Role of Women in Economic Development, World Bank, 1989; K. Staudt, "The Effects of Government Agricultural Policy on Women Farmers: Preliminary Findings from Idakho Location in Kakamega District, Institute of Development Studies, Nairobi, 1975; Kathleen Staudt, "Women Farmers and Inequities in Agricultural Services," in Edna Bay, ed., Women and Work in Africa, Boulder: Westview, 1982; Wangari Maathai, "Kenya's Green Belt Movement, Ecological Movement Headed by Women," UNESCO Courier, March 1992; Carmen Diana Deere, "Rural Women and State Policy: The Latin American Agrarian Reform Experience," World Development, 13, 1037-1053, 1985; Carmen Diana Deere, "The Division of Labor by Sex in Agriculture: A Peruvian Case Study," Economic Development and Cultural Change, 795-812, 1982; Rekha Mehra, "Can Structural Adjustment Work for Women Farmers," Amer. J. Agr. Econ., 1440-1447, Dec. 1991; Jean M. Due and Christina H. Gladwin, "Impacts of Structural Adjustment Programs on African Women Farmers and Female Headed Households," Amer. J. Agr. Econ., 1431-1439, Dec. 1991; David E. Sahn and Lawrence Haddad, "The Gendered Impacts of Structural Adjustment Programs in Africa: Discussion," Amer. J. Agr. Econ., 1448-1451, Dec. 1991; Joachim von Braun, Commercialization of Smallholder Agriculture: Policy Requirements for Capturing Gains for the Malnourished Poor, Washington, International Food Policy Research Institute, 1989; Christina H. Gladwin and Della McMillan, "Is a Turnaround in Africa Possible without Helping African Women to Farm?" Economic Development and Cultural Change, 345-369, 1989.

10. Environment, Debt and Development: Deforestation in the Brazilian Amazon Rain Forest

In recent years development specialists have made a major shift of focus towards problems of environment and development. Out of this, the theme of "sustainable development" emerged as a rallying point. It has been defined as "meeting needs of the present generation without compromising the needs of future generations," or as "development with respect for the natural world on which society and economy depend."

The idea of sustainable development may not offer anything qualitatively new to economic development analysis, but rather helps ensure that important existing ideas will be brought to the fore. Sustainable development is partly embodied in previously available economic concepts, especially using an appropriate social discount rate, a correct valuation of the environment as a capital stock rather than a free flow of consumption, and the proper internalization of negative environment and health externalities of projects.

But sustainability offers a clearer definition of development, in which future as well as current welfare and its distribution across generations is stressed. The value of the idea is shown by the fact that the term now has non-environmental uses such as whether a project continues on its own steam after foreign aid ends, and the extent of actual technology transfer including innovative capacity. Further, the term "sustainable development" has also served to coalesce a research agenda and concentrate policy makers' agendas. Even if it is no more than a glorified "bumper sticker," sustainable development is useful for that alone.

There is a close connection between poverty and environmental degradation. This comes as a surprise to many students and in fact it was perhaps initially unexpected by much of the profession. It is a commonly made conjecture that the richest billion and poorest billion people do the most environmental damage; the poorest billion probably do more damage than the middle 3.5 billion together and, depending on the weights placed on different types of environmental damage, they may even do more damage than the richest billion.

There are at least five important aspects of this poverty-environmental damage connection.

1) The high fertility of the absolutely poor and the threat to the environment of high population growth.

2) The fact that when one will starve if one does not use savings there is no finite discount rate. The poorest are known to eat their next year's seed corn to avoid starvation now--this is a metaphor for the general problem.

3) That even if survival is not at stake when one has insecure land tenure rights as the relatively poor often do, there is an incentive to treat land as a short-term resource. Lack of access to credit can have the same effect.

4) That in Latin America especially (also in the Philippines and elsewhere) inefficiently unequal land distribution produces political incentives to encourage poor farmers to establish inefficient rainforest settlements.

5) Perhaps most important, poverty is closely linked with the low status of women, who often have roles as guardians of natural resources, are responsible for agriculture, especially marginal agriculture, and have an ultimate responsibility for fertility.

At the macro level, there is also a close connection between the debt crisis and environmental degradation. The debt crisis 1) means LDCs cannot afford to import cleaner technologies; 2) creates a force for very high discount rates; and 3) this in turn encourages a shift from manufactures diversification to intensive natural resource extraction, which is often worse in total environmental impact than industry, especially when it degrades rainforests.

There is an important case to be made for new environment oriented foreign aid, as benefits of maintaining rainforests--in particular to alleviate the greenhouse effect and preserve biodiversity--go in large part to the developed world.

In a real sense, environmental degradation is like consumption out of the nation's capital stock. Increases in physical capital that may accompany destruction of environmental capital are often viewed as much less than compensating for its loss. One important outcome of the sustainable development theme is the extension by Robert Repetto and others of social accounting analysis to include environmental accounting. But it must be said that our ability to put a precise valuation on the loss of rain forest is still very primitive. There are no markets for the public goods and values for future generations that are at the source of the controversy over deforestation. Values must be imputed, and differences of opinion are inevitable.

Deforestation of the Brazilian Amazon Rain Forest shows many of the conflicts between short- and long-term development goals. Deforestation has often represented nonrenewable resource extraction without attention to negative externalities and often benefiting from ill-conceived subsidies for grandiose showcase development projects (like "Plan 2010") which often lacked economic justification but were supported by development agencies. The encouragement of low-income farmers to move in this case to Rondonia was a politically inexpensive--but ecologically disastrous--alternative to land reform.

Some of the perverse government incentives have now been well-publicized. Land titles were awarded to settlers on the basis of forest area cleared, which provided incentive for rainforest burning even when no economic use was planned; tax breaks were given for using Amazon land for ranches, which led the wealthy to develop the region to save taxes rather than on the basis of economic merits--cattle ranching activities for which there was a negative real rate of return, before the value of ecological damage was even considered, became viable to investors on tax-saving grounds alone.

Hans Binswanger of the World Bank has recently analyzed several other Brazilian policies that encourage deforestation in the Amazon, including a land tax that gives benefits for converting forest to pasture and the availability of subsidized credit for ranching. The disastrous economic and social, as well as ecological, effects of the conversion of tropical forest to pasture in Brazil--and the fact that sound alternatives to using this land for pasture do exist--has been abundantly demonstrated in a recent volume of two dozen studies edited by Theodore Downing and his colleagues.

The case of deforestation and ecological devastation of Brazil's Amazon rain forest exemplifies these points. Rainforest loss is having negative consequences for long-term development goals of Brazil, as well as for world environment goals like reduction of global warming. It represents one of the most serious environment issues of the developing world. It is also a case that illustrates problems of sustainable development.

Economic activities in the Amazon have been based on nonrenewable resource extraction without attention to negative externalities and often benefiting from ill-conceived subsidies. Grandiose showcase development projects and schemes were the order of the day, like "Plan 2010" with its hydrodams and subsidized ore mining. Such projects often lacked economic justification but were all too quickly supported by development agencies. But today, Brazil and the development agencies are finally beginning to take a new approach toward Amazon development.

The Amazon tropical rain forest is the world's largest rain forest, covering approximately 5 million square kilometers of land. The Amazon River basin covers 7 million square kilometers, making it the largest river drainage system on earth. Its diversity of plant and animal life is unmatched anywhere in the world. Almost three quarters of the Amazon rain forest is located in Brazil; about 1.3 million kilometers of the rain forest are located in Peru, Venezuela, Colombia and Ecuador.

Deforestation in the Amazon had not represented a significant problem prior to the 1980s. But most estimates show the total of deforested Amazon lands having grown dramatically from 3 million hectares in 1975 to 60 million hectares in 1988--an area larger than France. Estimates of deforestation by 1993 are up to 100 million hectares, though one recent NASA study suggested that the annual rate of deforestation might be as little as one third of previous estimates, but the loss of biodiversity much higher than previously estimated.

In one important study, Anthony Anderson examined the rush to establish charcoal-consuming industries in the Amazon supplied primarily by local rainforests. He found that this expansion has been driven by generous government incentives; that prospects for effective forest management looked weak; and projected that over 1500 square kilometers of rainforest were likely to be destroyed each year as a result.

The northwest state of Rondonia has experienced the most devastation, beginning with the 1970s construction of roads to the area and the encouragement of low-income farmers to move there as a way of removing pressure for land reform. The results were disastrous. The settlers logged, and more often burned the forests; the wealthy grazed cattle and the poor planted crops.

Rainforest soils are well-known to be fragile. Most nutrients in rainforest ecologies are in the biomass itself, and are lost when a rainforest is burned. As the soils became quickly depleted, new forests were cleared, in a form of non-renewable slash and burn agriculture. The use of tree crops rather than annual crops was not encouraged in the tax code, despite its positive externalities and sustainability benefits, and so soils were depleted all the faster.

In addition to rainforest loss, water resources were contaminated on a vast scale for downstream users, including erosion and siltation, and the spread of waterborne disease. Most egregiously, rights of indigenous peoples were flagrantly violated, with terrible atrocities committed by settlers. Ecological campaigners and activists among rubber-tappers whose livelihoods were threatened were attacked and sometimes murdered, as Francisco "Chico" Mendes was in 1988.

The World Bank was partly responsible for this calamity. For example, it funded the paved, all-weather highway from the region to Porto Velho and other Rondonia projects. This facilitated haphazard settlement of the area, including agriculture on fragile lands that quickly went barren. As Brent Millikan has described, some of the projects had nominal environmental protection components, but they were not enforced.

After intense pressure from environmental groups and concerned donor governments, the Bank stopped direct lending support for these ill-conceived Rondonian settlements. The Bank also funded the vast Carajas Iron Ore project, which led to the environmental devastation of Para State, the costs of which were barely taken into account in project calculations and the balance sheets of participating companies.

These Amazon experiences and the resulting public outcry were also largely responsible for the establishment of the Environment Division of the World Bank and other reforms announced in a 1987 speech by World Bank President Barber Conable.

In the late 1980s, Brazil began to reverse its perverse Amazon incentives. Incentives for clearing Amazon land were sharply reduced. Publicly funded roadbuilding in ecologically fragile regions was greatly scaled back. After some pressure on Brazil, in 1992 the Rondonia Natural Resources Management Project (RNRMP) was introduced in an attempt to rectify these problems. The environmentally conscious RNRMP has earned high marks from environment and development specialists. As part of the plan, Indian reservations have been increased in size. Land titles are denied to settlers in prohibited zones. Several nature parks and biological reserves have been established. Land use planning has been rationalized through the use of in-depth satellite imaging, financed by the World Bank. The results confirmed that only a little over 10% of Rondonia's area (about 2.6 out of 24.3 million hectares) could support sustainable annual crop use. An additional 6.4 million hectares was determined to be capable of sustainable tree crop use (notably rubber, coffee and fruit).

Avenues for public participation in land use decisions have been created in Brazil. The World Bank has increasingly demanded better legal protection for Indian rights. Certain "extractive reserves" have been established, like a 1.1 million acre reserve in Jari State established in 1990, on which 2500 families live and engage in practices like rubber tapping.

All of these changes have been helpful. But enforcement of the new rules has been difficult and poachers have continued their activities. Some of the loss of vital rainforest lands and other ecological damage may prove irreversible. In a certain sense deforestation has gathered a momentum of its own. Now that critical initial investments have been made and economic activities have reached significant returns to scale, the once-crucial public subsidies are no longer needed for various activities and the private sector has found it can operate profitably on its own--provided investors do not have to pay for the environmental damage they cause. For example, as Anthony Anderson reports, ranchers in the state of Para are constructing their own private road to the adjacent state of Marahao, to extract timber.

It is essential that more be done. The first need is for more research. Further attention to alternative uses, such as "eco-tourism," should be given. Forest management in other tropical rainforests has led to extremely high, profitable--and sustainable--fruit yields. Products that can be harvested without serious ecological disruption include fibers, latex, resins, gums, medicines, and game.

Some environmental advocates seem to have implied that people should continue practicing low productivity, low income traditional gathering activities indefinitely. But research can yield newer techniques and products that will support use of the rain forest in an ecologically sustainable manner. Another recent collection of studies, Alternatives to Deforestation, has demonstrated that higher productivity practices are feasible--and sustainable. Support to further such research should be given a high priority.

Poor peasants are often blamed for a significant part of deforestation for their slash and burn agricultural practices. This is in fact a major proximate cause of the problem, but this is more like blaming the victim than a useful basis for policy. The poor move to the Amazon and practice ecologically harmful agriculture once they get there because they are lacking in resources. Land reform benefiting poor farmers and financial credit, extension, and other services for the poor once they get access to land should be a top priority.

Moreover, since the rest of the world benefits from Brazil's rain forests through prevention of global warming, ecological cleansing, and irreplaceable biodiversity needed for future antibiotics other medicines and goods, the world should be prepared to pay something to ensure its continuation. Financial support as well as political pressure for land reform is one clear direction. Debt for nature swaps would seem an important avenue for this, but unlike some other Amazon countries like Bolivia, Brazil has traditionally resisted these swaps on the grounds that they infringe on sovereignty. Yet with imagination there must be some way to accomplish the same end. Recently Brazil has been participating in talks designed to do just that.

Sources: The World Bank World Development Report 1992, "Development and the Environment," New York: Oxford; Environment and Development in Latin America and the Caribbean: The Role of the World Bank, World Bank, 1992; Funding Ecological and Social Destruction: The World Bank and The IMF, Bank Information Center, Washington DC, 1990; Washington Post, May 31, 1992 and June 25, 1993; Robert Repetto et al, Wasting Assets, Natural Resources in the National Income Accounts, Washington: World Resources Institute, 1989; Anthony B. Anderson, "Smokestacks in the Rainforest: Industrial Development and Deforestation in the Amazon Basin, World Development, 18, 9, 1191-1205 (1990); Anthony B. Anderson, ed., Alternatives to Deforestation, New York: Columbia, 1990; Brent Millikan, "Land Degradation, Deforestation, and Society," Latin American Perspectives, 19,1, 45-72, 1992; Theodore E. Downing et al, eds., Development or Destruction: The Conversion of Tropical Forest to Pasture in Latin America, Boulder: Westview, 1992; David Goodman and Anthony Hall, eds., The Future of Amazonia, New York: St. Martins, 1990; Hans P. Binswanger, "Brazilian Policies that Encourage Deforestation in the Amazon, World Development, 19, 7, 821-829, 1991; "Mining in the Amazonian Rainforests," Nature, Feb. 1992, p. 593-594.

11. The Many Development Benefits of Educating Girls: Pakistan

In the 1992 Quad-i-Azam lecture to the Pakistan Society of Development Economists, Larry Summers, then chief economist of the World Bank, argued that giving 100 girls one additional year of primary education would prevent roughly 60 infant deaths and 3 maternal deaths, while averting some 500 births. Drawing on earlier World Bank sponsored research, he argued that programs to increase female education are less expensive than other development investments, at a cost of some $30,000 for 100 girls. This is actually a conservative estimate because it is based on secondary school cost and primary school costs are lower. Summers concluded that the social benefits alone of increased education of girls is more than sufficient to cover its costs--even before considering the added earnings power this education would bring.

The World Bank's focus on girls' education is part of a broad evolution of attitudes about the role of women in development, and the unacceptability of continuing to treat educational discrimination against females as a sovereign cultural matter outside of the purview of development agencies. In this study we look more deeply at the case of Pakistan, to better appreciate the reasons for this.

Girls receive significantly less education, health care, and other resources needed for a productive and successful life than do boys. This pattern repeats itself generation after generation. Of course, this is patently unfair. It is hard to see how apologetics by cultural relativists who say Western values of gender equality should not be imposed on Third World societies are ultimately meaningful in cases such as this. But the repercussions from the efficiency point of view are as serious as the equity repercussions, and this case study is about the economic rather than the social development implications of gender inequality.

In Pakistan, girls face perhaps more relative deprivation in comparison to boys than any other Asian country, and possibly as much as anywhere else in the world. It has been found to be one of the countries in which boys are most favored by parents over girls, along with Bangladesh, Jordan, Nepal, South Korea and Syria.

In Africa, women are often seriously disadvantaged relative to men, but both men and women are often in absolute poverty. Pakistan is thus a case in which the "gender gap" as a <u>relative</u> hardship can be seen very vividly.

Based on a 1981 census, the Government of Pakistan acknowledges that just 16% of women are literate (and 26% of the total population including men and women.)

Recently published statistics show that these numbers have barely moved to 19% and 30% respectively after a decade of efforts. Far too few of the young are receiving an education sufficient to pull up this figure any faster. UNESCO data show that only one-third of primary school age children and an even smaller percentage of girls in Pakistan are enrolled in school.

Just 1.7% of GNP is allocated to education; and this small allocation is extremely inequitable. Thirty times as many public education dollars are spent per pupil for university education as for primary school education; and that is an average: primary school expenditures are extremely unequal, with the lion's share of funds going to schools that more often train the few students who will eventually go on to universities. Discrimination and limited opportunities affect the poorest rural Pakistani girls the most and seem to affect the daughters of the urban elite little if at all. Poor girls lack the political voice to demand action for their problems.

While Pakistan has been receiving more than $1 billion annually in development assistance for its primary schools, only a fraction actually reaches the rural schools where it could make the most difference. As in most developing countries, poverty in Pakistan is concentrated in rural areas. Over two-thirds of Pakistan's population is still rural. This is where problems of undereducation, especially for girls, are overwhelmingly concentrated. Today while 55.3% of urban males are literate, the corresponding share of rural females is just 7.3%. Women also often have greater difficulty in practicing and maintaining their hard-won literacy skills than men. Reading materials are generally not designed for the interests or needs of women, when they are available to them at all.

Problems for poor girls in rural areas do not begin or end with undereducation, though most other problems are closely related to it. One of the most serious problems afflicting poor children is diarrhea. It accounts for a large percentage of deaths before age 5. Even with good food availability, chronic childhood diarrhea leads to malnutrition and long-term health problems even where it is not fatal in the short-run. Girls are differentially affected because studies show they are less likely to receive medical attention than boys.

Inferior health care access for girls shows the interlinked nature of economic incentives and cultural milieu. The parents may be perceived as behaving rationally according to the economic incentives and constraints they face. A boy provides future economic benefits, such as support in old age, receipt of a dowry upon marriage, and often continued work on the farm into adulthood. A girl, in contrast, will require a dowry upon marriage, often at a young age, and will then move to the village of the husband's family, becoming responsible for the welfare of the husband's parents. A girl from a poor rural Pakistani family will perceive no suitable alternatives in life to serving a husband.

To a poor family, the income value of children is substantial and consequential. Treatment of disease may be expensive and may require several days lost from work to go to the town. Empirical studies demonstrate what we might guess from these perverse incentives: much more strenuous efforts are made to save the life of a son than a daughter.

It is well known that fertility is inversely related to years of mothers' schooling. The usual interpretation is that mothers with more schooling have a higher "opportunity cost of childrearing," or higher potential wages that they give up to devote time to bearing another child. Poverty encourages high fertility, and high population growth hinders development in an "endogenous" vicious circle. The evidence suggests that despite discrimination and frequently lower wages for women who do work comparable to men, the percentage returns to additional schooling is similar for males and females in developing countries. These returns are between 10% and 25% in most developing countries, and by most estimates are on the high part of this range in Pakistan. These impressive returns alone justify expanding educational opportunities.

There is some limited evidence that population growth may actually increase up to the first approximately four years of education. The explanation is that a woman has learned enough in school to take better care of basic nutrition and health, so that the number of surviving children will rise to its higher, desired level. In any case, after four years of schooling, the desired level itself seems to fall. Recently, the United Nations has begun to push for a minimum six years of schooling for all children.

Returns are generally highest at the earliest years of schooling. Since girls receive less education than boys, if any at all, taken together this makes the case for special emphasis on increasing years of schooling for girls. Yet more than two thirds of primary school dropouts in Pakistan are girls. Keep in mind that these wage benefits are not even part of the calculations of health and other social benefits considered above.

The smaller the family, the more resources each child receives on average. And in most countries at most points in economic history, rapid population growth hinders development. Here the benefits of expanded education of girls is plain.

Education might improve prospects for the daughter's welfare. Studies show that mothers' education plays a decisive role in raising nutritional levels in rural areas. The level of child stunting, a valid indicator of child undernutrition, is much lower with higher education attainment of the mother, at any given income level. Harold Alderman and Marito Garcia report evidence that projects that the incidence of child stunting would be reduced by a quarter of current levels (from 63.6% to 47.1%) if women were to attain a primary level education. They note that this is almost ten times the projected impact of a 10% increase in per capita income. Coupled with the result that in many countries mothers education tends to makes a disproportionately larger health difference toward daughters than sons, as Duncan Thomas has reported, we can expect major benefits for girls.

Such conditions help explain the "missing women mystery." In Asia, the United Nations has found that there are far fewer females as a share of the population than would be predicted by demographic norms. In developed countries there are about 105 girls for every 100 boys. Worldwide as many as 100 million women are "missing." But in Asia there are about 110 boys for every 100 girls, an average pulled up by the infamous case of China, where the rate is about 115 to 100. In Pakistan, the rate is about 109 to 100. Reasons include female infanticide and selective abortion, but a larger part of the explanation is poorer treatment of women after birth.

What can be done? Some small steps are easy. Increasing the available information on gender discrimination will have direct and indirect effects. Development professionals need to begin to collect information on gender differences in development much more systematically, and to warn health and social workers to be alert for effects of gender discrimination.

Some programs have had some success. Literacy programs in the province of Baluchistan have been hampered by the wide distances between villages--about 50 miles on average. Only about 2600 of the 5800 villages in the region even have a primary school.

In many areas it is considered improper for a male teacher to teach female students. On the other hand, due to the lack of schooling opportunities the rate of female literacy is so low it can be hard to find female teachers. This classic Catch-22 will be a difficult paradox to resolve.

In addition to the need for female teachers, there is a related shortage of female agricultural extension workers. In rural Pakistan, women are often actively involved in farming, but almost all extension agents are male, who for cultural reasons are often unable or unwilling to train women. Female agents must be trained, but even assuming the government has the will to address this problem, literate women capable of filling this role can be hard to find. There is a stigma in rural Pakistan against women working in the fields; and many poorer families simply deny that women and girls are working at all. Again, we seem confronted with a Catch-22.

Other steps are harder. It would certainly help to abolish dowries and other practices that unnecessarily increase the cost of raising girls. But this is much easier to legislate than enforce. The creation of a viable pension system, such as South Korea has established would help to change the perception that sons are much more worthwhile because they alone can provide financially for parents in old age.

In recent years the government of Pakistan has made some efforts to promote female literacy. But despite all the attention and pressure on the issue, progress continues to be painfully slow. The Bhutto government decided that it had to back down from its earlier lofty goal of attaining 90% literacy to providing educational infrastructure that could serve all children age 5 to 9. This was intended to reduce urban bias as well as lower barriers to girls' education. This goal remains far in the future. The government is also trying to get the private sector involved, but this too will have small impact on rural areas.

The case for stressing girls' education is so strong it may be hard to see why action is not forthcoming, especially now that top government leaders are at least paying lip service to the problem. One reason is that while girls' education is a boon for development as a whole, it is not necessarily in the economic and political interests of some of those now in powerful positions, especially at a more local or regional level.

In rural areas of Pakistan, as elsewhere in South Asia and the Middle East, landlords gain from peasants from "extraeconomic coercion" as well as from free and honest exchange. In sweatshops, laws on such matters as child labor and fire safety are regularly disregarded. Workplace rights problems in the US on such matters as sexual harassment and the right to unionize seem very mild compared to the abuses that go on in fields and workplaces in this part of the world.

With education, some landlords and industrialists know well, workers, and especially women, may finally demand that laws already in place ostensibly to protect them be enforced. It is in their business interest--as well as in their self-interest more generally--to see that this does not happen.

In this the landlords and industrialists often have allies in groups like the local religious leaders, who view women's education as a cultural threat. Seclusion of girls and women remains widespread in rural areas. Many male heads of households will prevent their daughters from becoming educated or their wives from gaining literacy because they fear their loss of power at home, or fear ostracization by peers who feel more threatened than they. Rural girls see that women reaching marriage age often have difficulty finding a husband if they are literate--a powerful disincentive to education. The ongoing "Islamization" movement, as it has unfolded so far, is viewed by United Nations observers as not helpful to the advancement of education of girls.

Not surprisingly in this climate, a womens' rights movement has been growing in Pakistan. There is an active debate over whether Islamic fundamentalists' position on women represents a "biased" reading of the Koran. The growth of a women's movement must be treated as a good sign, because without the kind of political pressure such a movement can engender, it is doubtful whether the harder steps will be taken any time soon. Even so, the huge gulf between urban and rural Pakistan will be difficult to cross.

Sources. "Pakistan Faces Obstacles to Literacy," Christian Science Monitor, Oct. 28, 1991; Katrin Saito, Extending Help to Women Farmers in LDCs," Finance and Development, Sept. 1991; Duncan Thomas, Gender Differences in Household Resource Allocations, World Bank Living Standards Measurement Study Paper 79; Harold Alderman and Marito Garcia, "Food Security and Health Security: Explaining the Levels of Nutrition in Pakistan," World Bank Working Paper PRE 865, 1992; Larry Summers, "Investing in All the People, World Bank Working Paper PRE 905, 1992; "Daughters are Disadvantaged from Birth," World Health, June 1986; Sundari Ravindran, "Health Implications of Sex Discrimination in Childhood," Netherlands: International Statistical Institute; Neelam Hussain, "Women and Literacy Development in Pakistan," undated working paper; Agneta Lind, "The Gender Gap. Women: One Billion Illiterates," UNESCO Courier, 1990; Hugh Courtney and Stephen C. Smith "Growth and the Distribution of Human Capital Investment: Theory and Cross-National Evidence," George Washington U. Economics Discussion Paper 9314, 1993.

12. NAFTA and Beyond: Impact on Mexico and Latin America

In mid-1990, President Carlos Salinas de Gotari of Mexico and then-US President George Bush agreed to pursue negotiations toward a North American Free Trade Agreement (NAFTA). Negotiations proceeded quickly and at the end of 1992, the US, Canada and Mexico signed a draft NAFTA accord, which is intended to become law on Jan. 1, 1994, after ratification by each country's legislature and the working out of certain side agreements on labor and environmental standards.

The proposed agreement is of enormous consequence not only for Mexico, the second-largest Latin American economy, but in the precedent it sets for development opportunities and dilemmas throughout the Third World. NAFTA would be the first free trade agreement between developed and developing countries, and so will play a crucial role in defining the future policy debate on trade and the developing countries.

NAFTA would eliminate all tariff barriers and most nontariff barriers between the three countries within 10 years, though a few products would be given a 15-year transition period. It would include free trade in agricultural products, a frequent stumbling block in trade accords. Mexico would be able to export textiles and apparel to the US and Canada without the protectionist restrictions of the multifiber agreement that limit textile exports from many other developing countries. NAFTA would largely open up financial services markets, as well as telecommunications and transportation services markets. Foreign investors from the three signing countries investing in other NAFTA countries would receive legal treatment equal to that of local investors in each country.

The debate over NAFTA in Mexico mirrors the longstanding debate about advantages and disadvantages of free trade with developed countries for developing countries' economic prospects.
Free trade critics have doubted expected growth for primary exports because of low income elasticities of these static comparative advantage goods, also associated with secular deterioration of terms of trade. They equate modern economies and modern economic growth with industrialization, and fear that free trade would induce them to specialize in goods with low long-term productivity growth. However, the objection to free trade that first world protectionism is substantial and appears to be on the rise would appear to be obviated by a genuine free trade pact.

Free trade proponents expect exports to grow and lead economic growth, arguing that free trade improves resource allocation, eliminates distortions, promotes efficiency, raises domestic and foreign savings, and generates foreign exchange. Certainly, neither side is always correct; it depends on world economic conditions such as protectionism, and on the ability of a developing country to carry out an efficient industrialization strategy.

To date the development literature specifically on economic integration, as opposed to free trade generally, is concentrated on free trade areas among developing countries. There is also a large general literature on integration and on common markets among developed countries. Proponents argue that free trade areas provide dynamic creation of new industries, economies of scale, and possibilities of coordinated industrial policy as well as static trade creation. Many analysts argue that free trade areas are beneficial to the extent that they "create" trade, but detrimental to the extent that they "divert" trade that would have taken place with other countries that might have a more appropriate comparative advantage.

For example, the NAFTA rules are expected to lead to a diversion of trade in textiles to Mexico and away from other developing countries. However, some analysts argue that even trade diversion may provide development benefits when seen in a dynamic perspective, along the lines of the "infant industry argument" that developing countries just need some time to get efficient industries on their feet.

A desire to lower debt burdens is the driving impulse for Mexico and other LDCs to join the free trade agreement bandwagon. FTAs will attract direct foreign investment, or at least keep it from getting diverted to other countries that do set up such agreements. FTAs may be perceived as a kind of insurance against the United States setting up new trade restrictions. The United States is already by far the largest importer of Mexican goods, and Mexican business and political leaders hope for NAFTA to build on this base. Other Latin American countries, led by Chile, seem eager to join in a broader regional free trade agreement as soon as possible.

Despite disclaimers, the Mexican government would like nothing more than to hear the sweet sound of Ross Perot's "giant sucking machine," transporting formerly American jobs to Mexico: that is their job. Other Latin American countries will try to enter NAFTA, in part out of fear of losing diverted trade to Mexico. But even if all of Latin America were to set up free trade agreements with the US, most of the benefits would probably still go to Mexico, at least until Mexican wages rose substantially, due primarily to its location on the US border.

Investment has already been pouring into Mexico since negotiations on the treaty began, anticipating a Jan. 1, 1994 free trade area--just as investments increased in European Community countries leading up to the more ambitious Jan. 1, 1993 completion of the single internal European market. Depending on how they are measured, inflows of capital to Mexico amounted to about 8.5% of GDP in 1992, or over $20 billion, and are projected to reach similar levels in 1993.

Some studies have been very optimistic about the impact on Mexico. The North American Free Trade Area is projected to create some 600,000 jobs in Mexico, according to an Institute for International Economics analysis. Unemployment was very high in Mexico in the mid-1980s, reaching about 18% in 1986-87. By 1991, the official figure had fallen to just 2.7%. As usual, it is hard to interpret LDC unemployment figures. Underemployment is generally much higher, and Mexican underemployment rates have been estimated at 25-40%. This latter figure underscores the concern over jobs in Mexico. Moreover, Mexico has a dramatic age pyramid, with some 10 times the number of young workers entering the labor force as old workers retiring.

The potential downside for Mexico is not obvious at first glance. Most developing countries including those in Latin America are viewing Mexico's prospective open access to the world's largest economy with envy. Economies such as Taiwan whose development has been fueled by exports to the United States are extremely concerned about the potential loss of business to Mexico. One concern is over the possible erosion of import substitution firms which may not be able to stand up to US competition.

Studies by Michael Porter and others strongly suggest that the presence of domestic owned and based firms is very important in securing long-term economic development. Free trade agreements can inhibit rather than encourage the development of indigenous industrial capacities. For this reason critics Robert Pastor and Jorje Castenada have raised the specter of Mexico becoming "a nation of maquiladoras, dishwashers, US welfare recipients, and hotel help, condemned to produce the few goods for which it has a significant comparative advantage."

The history of NAFTA does begin in 1965 with the maquiladoras industries on the U.S. border. In the last half of the 1980s, maquiladoras industries have been estimated to be responsible for some 84% of Mexico's economic growth. Today over 2000 plants, most of which are located in the Mexican border states, employ over 500,000 workers.

The late 1980s was also a period which saw the beginning of upgrading the types of labor performed there. Still, no more than 20% of the maquiladoras' chief executive officer positions are filled by Mexican nationals. Most of the rest are Americans, many of whom live north of the border. But while some 87% of maquiladoras are on border states, those that are located further south tend to have Mexican CEOs, and the prospect of this becoming more the norm is clearly one selling point of NAFTA to the Mexican government.

Mexico has traditionally wished to avoid dependence on the United States for its development. There have been nationalist tensions between the two countries since the US-Mexican war nearly 150 years ago.

Mexico's highly protectionist development strategy with its active use of state owned enterprises (SOEs) throughout most of this century evolved in significant part to assure economic independence from the enormous US economy to the North. Industrialization was always seen as the key to economic autonomy. But industrialization requires industrial knowhow and capital. Earlier, the intention was for these to be accumulated internally through learning by doing and savings generated through taxes and profits of state-owned enterprises.

Despite the disappointments of SOE inefficiency, this stress on autonomy was reinforced when large new oil reserves were proven. But the overhang of the debt crisis, continued inefficiency and falling oil prices in the 1980s showed that a role for foreign capital would be needed. Before NAFTA was agreed to, Mexico went to some lengths to push for expanded Japanese and European investment, including major promotional tours of Japan and the European Community in 1990 by President Salinas. But with the world seemingly coalescing into regional trading groups, and great doubts about the plausibility of large-scale European and Japanese investments in Mexico, it became clear that an arrangement would first have to be reached with the US.

Even so, in some ways NAFTA represents a change in Mexican industrialization tactics more than in development strategy. The goal is still to make Mexico an important industrial power. In abandoning the Latin American inward-looking development model, Mexico seems to wish to copy the state-led development strategy of East Asia rather than the pure free market model. As in East Asia, the state is getting out of productive activity, but retains a strong hand in guiding that activity toward a more sophisticated skill and technology content.

While Mexico's leaders realized that investments would have to come first from the US, they have not given up on special arrangements with Europe and Japan. Mexican foreign minister Fernando Solana said in Europe in April 1993 that after NAFTA is ratified Mexico will seek a special trade accord with the European Community.

Issues of labor rights and environmental protection will be at the center of final negotiations. Mexico and the United States are currently negotiating "side accords" intended to ensure that firms do not move to Mexico only to avoid environmental or job safety responsibility and that Mexican labor and environmental laws are enforced. In principle, such side accords should benefit the public interest in both countries.

Gene Grossman and Alan Krueger have suggested that Mexico's environment will be helped by NAFTA. They have found some evidence for an "inverted U" relationship between income per capita and pollution. As income rises, pollution rises until upper middle income levels are reached; then it begins to fall as societies become willing and able to pay for environmental protection. Grossman and Krueger argue that NAFTA will increase income in Mexico so much that Mexico will start to pay for pollution clean-up without outside prompting (or in other words move to the downward-sloping side of this curve). But American negotiators are unwilling to take this on faith, and environmental side agreements are certain to be adopted if NAFTA is to be accepted in the United States.

Part of the motivation for Mexican leaders is to keep Mexico committed to the free market, liberalization strategy they have been pursuing since the mid-1980s. NAFTA codifies many of the liberalization measures undertaken by Salinas. As an international treaty, NAFTA would be hard for a subsequent administration to overturn.

Mexican officials hope that NAFTA will result in higher Mexican wages, and economic theory offers support for this idea. The factor price equalization theorem predicts that free trade will equalize wages of the various skill types across two free-trading regions. Evidence for this is mixed, partly because it is not clear how close conditions have to be to free trade for this to occur at any given speed. Given Mexico's large and growing, often underemployed unskilled workforce--some two-thirds of the total--it is hard to believe unskilled workers' wages can rise quickly. Unskilled wages in America, on the other hand, may more likely continue to fall.

On the other hand, skilled workers' wages in Mexico are already increasing rapidly. Evidence from the European Community supports the idea of wage convergence in a free trade area. In dollar terms, Mexican wages are up from just $1 per hour to over $2.50 per hour in the six years from 1987-93. American wages have hardly budged in this period. The apparent Mexican gain is in significant part because of the fall of the value of the dollar in this period. Part of this increase in Mexican wages also reflects the internal economic recovery from the depths of recession. However calculated, when adjusted for purchasing power parity the rise is still present but is much smaller. It is too early to say anything conclusive about rapid convergence of Mexican and US wages.

The case of Puerto Rico, which has had effective free trade with the US for decades, provides limited support for both supporters' and critics' concerns. Certainly wages have risen more rapidly in Puerto Rico than elsewhere in Latin America, but as noted by Hufbauer and Schott, wages remain at about half US levels. There has been no flood of investment from the US or other countries; unemployment in Puerto Rico remains extremely high even by Latin American standards, and less than 15% of the workforce have manufacturing jobs, fewer than 20 years ago. Moreover, dependence on US companies and investments is almost total, and indigenous Puerto Rican corporations have not become even a tiny factor in the world economy. Nor has Puerto Rico's innovation capacity grown much. Puerto Rico may have benefitted from short-run income gains at the expense of long-run development.

But Puerto Rico's true alternative might have been much worse. Without its close ties to the American economy, the island of Puerto Rico might well have been more a Dominican Republic than a Japan. Its per capita GNP in 1985 was about $4500, about twice that of Korea. One must always evaluate a policy against the true next-best alternative, not against an imagined ideal. More than anything Puerto Rico seems to suggest the unspectacular nature of free-trade agreements. The impact, whether more a long-run spur or hinderance to true development, is likely to be modest in size.

Finally, we have the vexing question of whether NAFTA would strengthen or weaken the world trading system? If regional free trade agreements are just a more realistic stepping stone toward an ultimately freer world trade regime, NAFTA will help. But if it is seen as an end in itself and an alternative to trade with other regions, NAFTA could do much to speed the trend toward a system of trading blocks. The Institute for International Economics has concluded that without strong GATT reforms, NAFTA could be trade diverting rather than trade creating. If some developing countries end up privileged by the new system and others left out in the cold, the results could be a net negative for development prospects.

In sum, we can be sure that NAFTA offers Mexico the opportunity for employment creation. As to whether it carries its other touted benefits, or carries risks of restraints on future development, either for Mexico or for developing countries left out of such special arrangements--this remains to be seen.

Sources: "The Mexican Worker: " Business Week cover story; Clyde Prestowitz et al, The New North American Order: A Win-Win Strategy for US-Mexico Trade, Economic Strategy Inst., 1991; Institute for International Economics, various documents; Refik Erzan, Free Trade Agreements with the United States: What's in it for Latin America?" World Bank Policy Research Working Paper 827, 1992; Stephen C. Smith, Industrial Policy in Developing Countries: Reconsidering the Real Sources of Export Led Growth, 1991, M.E.Sharpe for Economic Policy Institute, James Russell Meade, The Low-Wage Challenge to Global Growth: The Labor Cost-Productivity Imbalance in Newly Industrialized Countries, 1991, M.E.Sharpe for Economic Policy Institute; Robert F. Pastor and Jorje G. Castenada, Limits to Friendship: The United States and Mexico, New York: Vintage, 1988; US Dept. of Labor Bureau of International Labor Affairs, Foreign Labor Trends, various issues; Michael Porter, Competitive Advantage of Nations, (NY: Free Press, 1990); Rhee, Yung Whee, Bruce Ross-Larson and Gary Pursell, Korea's Competitive Edge: Managing the Entry into World Markets, Baltimore: Johns Hopkins for the World Bank, 1984; Westphal, Larry E., Yung W. Rhee and Gary Pursell, Korean Industrial Competence: Where it Came From, World Bank Staff Working Paper No. 469, 1981; Gary C. Hufbauer and Jeffrey J. Schott, North American Free Trade: Issues and Recommendations, Washington: Institute for International Economics, 1992; Gary C. Hufbauer and Jeffrey J. Schott, NAFTA: An Assessment, Washington: Institute for International Economics, 1993; Luis Pazos, Free Trade: Mexico-USA. Facts and Myths, Derachos Reservados, 1990; Khosrow Fatem, The Maquiladora Industry: Economic Solution or Problem, Mew York: Praeger, 1990; Statistical Abstract of the United States, 1992; Van R. Whiting, The Political Economy of Foreign Investment in Mexico: Nationalism, Liberalism and Constraints on Choice, Baltimore: Johns Hopkins, 1992.

13. Mexico: A pioneer in successful debt reduction

In August, 1982 Mexico triggered the Third World debt crisis when it announced that it could not pay its debt service, and would begin a moratorium of at least three months on debt payments to private creditors. Creditor banks, led by Citibank, formed an advisory committee. Mexico sought and received emergency assistance from the IMF and US financial institutions. In September, Mexico nationalized its banks and introduced total exchange controls.

In late September, the annual World Bank-IMF meetings took place in Toronto in what is frequently described as an atmosphere of panic. The greatest fear was that the stability of the international banking system was in peril, if significant defaults on loans threatened the major banks. The crisis swept through Latin America, Africa and other developing countries like the Philippines and Yugoslavia. A plan was devised that saved the banking system, but which led to what is often called the lost decade of development in Latin America and Africa.

Mexico was not only the first country to enter a debt crisis but a pacesetter in finding resolutions to it. This case study will examine the strategy it followed. It is largely based on the excellent book on the subject by Sudarshan Gooptu. The debt crisis has now been declared over by many observers, and the pioneering role played by Mexico has been an important part of recovery. But it may be premature to declare the crisis over and Mexico's case suggests how the seeds of new crisis could possibly be being sown anew.

The genesis of the debt crisis is well known. The oil shock of 1973 led to world recession. Developing countries like Mexico found their export markets smaller at the same time as they were faced with a larger oil bill. The price elasticity of oil in the short run is very small, and it was not easy to reduce the amount of oil imported without major economic dislocations.

For decades, it had been hard for Latin American countries to secure bank loans from major developed country banks; and before 1973, the external debt of Mexico, like most LDCs, was relatively small, primarily official, and often concessional lending. But major OPEC countries received a huge cash windfall from the 1973 oil price rise, and to sterilize this foreign exchange; they deposited much of the funds in major American banks. These banks had to lend the money to earn interest, out of which to pay interest to the OPEC depositors. Mexico and other Latin American countries had a ready demand for these loanable funds. Commercial banks, recycling petrodollars, began issuing general purpose loans to LDCs to provide balance of payments support and expansion of export sectors. From 1970 to 1992, Third World external debt grew from $68 to over $2000 billion. Debt service payments were over $169 billion in the early 1990s.

Mexico did not discover its substantial new oil reserves until later in the decade. Following Citibank Chairman John Reed's dictum that "sovereign countries do not default," large banks lent to this region with abandon, often overlooking normal criteria of country lending risk. Loans outstanding increased by 10 times in less than a decade.

Fate was sealed in the resulting crisis when Mexico and other borrowing countries failed to increase domestic investments apace with borrowing to levels capable of producing adequate levels of viable exports. Investment as a share of GDP hardly increased at all in this period of massive borrowing. This meant that Mexico and other borrower countries did not have the added capacity to produce the exports that could have generated foreign exchange to repay the debt without necessitating a fall in living standards.

Problems in Mexico were aggravated by very large fiscal deficits and inflation. After Mexico discovered additional large oil reserves and began producing oil in larger amounts in 1977, the country was merely tempted to borrow more money with oil as an implicit collateral. But this money, too, was not wisely invested, and the oil industry was operated with considerable inefficiency. Exchange rate appreciation hurt other exports (an example of "Dutch disease," in which exports of a commodity raise exchange rates and crowd out manufacturing and agricultural exports), and nonoil industries were neglected.

If the first oil shock triggered international lending through the combination of loan demand and recycling petrodollars which expanded the supply of loanable funds, the second oil shock in 1979 triggered a reversal of this process, as interest rates rose, stagnation reduced the demand for LDC exports, and already high debt levels made further borrowing to accommodate high oil prices all the more difficult. When real interest rates rose dramatically after 1979, Mexico's debt burden became untenable. In early 1982, Mexico's financial position began to deteriorate rapidly. The country needed to borrow some $20 billion that year to finance its existing loans and meet its expected deficit. As the year progressed, bank loans were harder to arrange and required a substantially higher interest rate. Inflation rose and a series of devaluations began. When the crisis finally broke in August it should not have come as a surprise.

For Mexico, the early years of the crisis were harsh. An economic adjustment program under the auspices of the IMF was initiated to restore economic order. Typical elements of IMF stabilization packages included liberalization of foreign exchange and import controls, devaluation, interest rate rises, deficit reduction, wage restrictions, decreased price controls, and general opening up of the economy. It was widely argued in Mexico, that this would lead to adjustment without growth, with negative development consequences. Indeed, this "austerity" program was much resented by Mexican leaders, but they saw no alternative.

This "IMF period" of the debt crisis had as its explicit objective saving the stability of the world financial system, and this meant ensuring the stability of the major money center banks. Mexicans and the Mexican economy were clearly suffering. Real income fell dramatically from 1982-85. The IMF was asked to provide funds under less stringent conditions. Their standard public relations reply was, "we are the fire department. You call us when your house is on fire. We are not the carpenter. You don't complain when we put an axe to your door or cause water damage with our hoses." But by 1985 it had become clear that while the fire was being contained, it was not going out. There had been some achievements. In particular, the public sector deficit fell from about 17% to 8% as a share of GDP. But there had been a dramatic fall in the level of GDP, and a rise in poverty and inequality.

By 1985, the position of the banks was stabilizing. They were substantially reducing their exposure in Third World debt in relation to their paid-up capital. The immediate crisis subsided somewhat in 1984 when a "multi-year rescheduling agreement" with foreign banks stretched out repayment terms for Mexico's debt. But growth showed no sign of resuming in Mexico or elsewhere among the heavily indebted countries. No new capital flows were forthcoming to heavily indebted countries, and it became clear that a new approach would be needed.

In 1985 the American Secretary of State James Baker introduced a new initiative which became known as the Baker plan. The idea was to get growth to resume in debtor countries, so they could "grow their way out of debt." Debt forgiveness was still a taboo subject. But new funds would be lent to indebted countries that would let growth resume, drawing on private banks, the World Bank, the IMF, and other sources. In return, Mexico and other indebted countries would introduce market reforms that should facilitate the use of new funds in a more efficient and growth-enhancing manner.

Mexico became one of the first countries to participate in the Baker Plan. Mexico agreed to a major debt restructuring and domestic economy reform program in June 1986 under the new finance minister Gustavo Petricioli. Commercial banks agreed to over $7 billion in loans and a new rescheduling agreement covering some $54 billion. In turn, the World Bank offered a loan of one-half billion dollars. This represented the entry of the World Bank into structural adjustment loans (SALs) as part of the Baker Plan. Previously such loans were seen as the exclusive province of the IMF, with the World Bank specializing in project lending.

The IMF also committed new funds. At this time, Mexico was being hurt severely by the big drop in the price of oil of the mid-1980s. The IMF agreed to a "special stand-by" agreement, in which it would make some $600 million credit available to Mexico in the eventuality that the price of oil fell below $9 a barrel. The IMF also offered substantial new credit, which was to be matched by new credits from commercial banks. Mexico did introduce far-reaching market-oriented reforms in this period. The most important reason why this approach did not work in the end is that commercial banks proved unwilling to "do their part" in net new lending.

Mexico had been one of the countries at the forefront of a major trend of the 1970s, limiting the allowed role of foreign multinational firms to participating only in approved minority joint ventures in most sectors. One effect of the debt crisis was that these restrictions were largely lifted. Full subsidiaries were allowed. The level of direct foreign investment (DFI) increased steadily.

In the mid-1980s Mexico became one of the pioneers of debt-equity swaps as an instrument of debt reduction. In these swaps, restrictions on DFI are lifted when foreign investors pay for the asset by presenting Mexican debt paper. These are acquired, usually at a substantial discount, from banks that wish to reduce their Third World debt exposure. The secondary market for Latin American debt has an average discount of perhaps 50% of face value (sometimes with far steeper discounts). The investor presents the loan to the central bank, which in turn issues local currency (pesos in the case of Mexico) which can be used only to purchase a local firm's assets. Sometimes the firm may be a state owned enterprise, so the transaction facilitates privatization. But debt equity swaps carry the inherent risk of generating inflationary pressures, since they usually involve swaps of public debt for private assets. Since it is the central bank that issues currency for the investor to buy a local asset, this represents a direct addition to high-powered money.

Mexico suspended debt-equity swaps in November, 1987, officially because of their inflationary effects. A part of the real reason may have been political pressures to limit the share of foreign ownership and control in the economy, though swaps of private debt for private equity continued to be permitted. In any case, concerns about large-scale foreign ownership would represent another limitation on the ability to use debt-equity swaps as a major element of a debt reduction program.

As the debt-equity swap strategy lost momentum, in 1988 Mexico pioneered a new approach to debt reduction. Mexico would exchange some of its outstanding debt, perceived as high-risk, for new debt called "Aztec Bonds," that would be backed by US Treasury bonds bought by Mexico and held in Washington as collateral. An auction would be held, in which banks would bid on how much discount on the face amount of their existing loans they would accept to get the new, more secure bonds. In March 1988, some $2.5 billion of bonds were exchanged for $3.6 billion in bank debt, an average discount of about 33%. A total of some $6.7 billion was offered by banks, but Mexico rejected some of these bids as offering too small a discount. If the results were disappointing in their magnitude, they represented an important innovation, which was built on later in the Brady Plan.

Eventually it became clear to all parties that substantial Mexican growth could not resume until its large debt burden was actually reduced, not just rescheduled. With the major US money center banks out of immediate danger after several years of reducing Third World exposure (notably their large additions to loan loss reserves in summer 1987) debt reduction could be considered without risk of financial panic. A debt reduction plan was floated by the new US Treasury Secretary, Nicholas Brady, in March 1989.

Mexico was the first country to negotiate debt reduction under the new "Brady plan." Banks were given three options: to exchange loans for floating rate bonds with collateral at a 35% discount; to exchange loans for bonds with the same par value but receiving a lower, fixed interest rate; or to lend new money to finance Mexican interest payments, keeping nominal value of the debt they were owed intact. In 1990, 49% of the banks exchanged some $22 billion in debt for lower-interest, fixed rate bonds, and 41% exchanged $20 billion in debt for the discounted floating rate bonds. This constituted Mexico's creditor banks' "revealed preferences" from among the options.

Provided that Mexico continues to successfully service this debt, the bonds on deposit in Washington as collateral will earn interest that Mexico will receive, which can eventually be used for debt reduction or investment. These exchanges saved Mexico payments of about $1.3 billion per year. From the banks' point of view, the tradeoff involved giving up higher yielding but higher risk debt for lower yielding but lower risk debt. Following Mexico's example, other countries reduced their required payments under the Brady plan, and the debt crisis went into remission.

Successful debt reduction, combined with market reforms and the prospects of the North American Free Trade Agreement (NAFTA) have returned net positive capital flows to Mexico. Capital inflows have soared in Mexico in the early 1990s. This has enabled Mexico to return to current account deficits. Inflows of capital to Mexico amounted to almost 8.5% of GDP in 1992, and are projected to reach similar levels in 1993. Current account deficits were over 6% in 1992 and are projected to be close to 8% in 1993. Mexico's trade deficit in 1992 was some $19 billion. Its net investment inflows were some $23 billion.

This capital inflow success raises the question of whether it could be sowing the seeds of renewed crisis. The OECD's 1992 study of Mexico, while generally optimistic, raised serious doubts about whether such inflows could be sustainable. Exports have not grown in recent years nearly as fast as imports. Mexican growth can be resumed with the stimulus of these large capital inflows, but over the longer term it cannot be sustained by them.

Certainly, there are some important differences from the 1970s. The fact that much of the current inflow is in the form of equity rather than debt itself means that a repayments crisis is less plausible. At the same time, foreign private investment tends to be extremely volatile, especially foreign stock market investments. Investments can pour out of a country as rapidly as they pour in, as Chile discovered in its financial crash of the early 1980s.

In any case, as before, there is a risk that living standards will be lower in the future if the inflows are not invested in ways that will promote higher exports. Published statistics do show that investment as a share of GDP is rising. Unfortunately, the way Mexican statistics are assembled makes it impossible to judge whether funds are going to the right investments. Some of what is being invested may not pay off in greater capacity for producing exportables. For example, some of the new investment is going into commercial and residential real estate.

In sum, if the crisis is defined as a threat to the large commercial banks, it is largely over. If defined as a threat to development prospects, for many developing countries, even for Mexico, it is not over. The fact that Mexico is borrowing in dollars to finance road construction--tolls would be paid in pesos --may be a symbol of a potential new phase of the debt crisis in the future.

Sources. Sudarshan Gooptu, Debt Reduction and Development: The Case of Mexico, Westport: Praeger, 1993; Financial Times, various issues since 1982 including July 30, 1992; Feb. 12 and March 29, 1993; "The Mexican Worker: Business Week cover story; Clyde Prestowitz et al, The New North American Order: A Win-Win Strategy for US-Mexico Trade, Economic Strategy Inst., 1991; Institute for International Economics, various documents; Refik Erzan, Free Trade Agreements with the United States: What's in it for Latin America?" World Bank Policy Research Working Paper 827, 1992; Stephen C. Smith, Industrial Policy in Developing Countries: Reconsidering the Real Sources of Export Led Growth, 1991, M.E.Sharpe for Economic Policy Institute, Robert F. Pastor and Jorje G. Castenada, Limits to Friendship: The United States and Mexico, New York: Vintage, 1988;

14. Industrial and Export Policy in South Korea

Many developing countries have conducted active industrial policies. Those of some countries have clearly been failures, such as India and Argentina. But industrial policy has not failed everywhere, and South Korea appears to be a good example of success.

While one can never absolutely prove cause and effect, one of the most important reasons for South Korea's remarkable industrial achievements appears to be the orientation of its industrial policy toward promotion of exports of increasingly sophisticated skill and technology content. Strong financial incentives for industrial firms to move up the ladder of skills and technology have been present in most of its policies.

There appear to be market failures in the transfer of technology from developing countries similar to those in innovation of original technology in developed countries. Policies which reward success in the export of goods a step up in technology and skill content provide a good match between policy goals, incentives to firms to meet those goals, and monitoring to make sure goals are really met before rewards are received--or are "incentive compatible." Specifically, firms get efficient feedback on whether their goods meet world price and quality standards by competing on world export markets; and governments can more easily ensure that rewards go to firms which really make and sell the intended number and quality of the required products (exports can be "counted on the dock," or are otherwise more observable than goods for the home market). These points are brought out with a close examination of the case of South Korea.

There have been at least 21 major types of export promotion oriented industrial policy interventions in South Korea. Only some of these policies have been in effect in any one industry and at any one time, and in the most recent years, effective subsidies have been considerably scaled back but not eliminated.

1. Currency undervaluation. The effective exchange rate (EER) for exporters was kept higher than that for importers. As early as 1964, South Korea's EER for exports was 281 and its EER for imports was 247 --not trade neutrality but a pro-export bias.

2. Preferential access to imported intermediate inputs needed for producing exports, with strict controls to prevent abuse. Since 1975, rebates are only received after documenting the completion of the exports.

3. Targeted infant industry protection as a first stage before launching an export drive.

South Korea has had high dispersion of effective rates of protection even with a relatively low average.

4. Tariff exemptions on inputs of capital goods needed in exporting activities. (This is a price incentive, while preferential access (#2) is based on quantity restriction.)

5. Tax breaks for domestic suppliers of inputs to exporting firms, which constitutes a domestic content incentive.

6. Domestic indirect tax exemptions for successful exporters.

7. Lower direct tax on income earned from exports.

8. Accelerated depreciation for exporters.

9. Import entitlement certificates (exemptions from import restrictions) linked directly to export levels. Korea has long maintained an extensive list of items generally prohibited for import, including both luxury goods and import substitution targets. Profitable exemptions from this prohibition have often been available for firms exporting specified goods having low profit margins.

10. Direct export subsidies for selected industries (no longer in use).

11. Monopoly rights granted to the firm first to achieve exports in targeted industries.

12. Subsidized interest rates for exporters.

13. Preferential credit access for exporters in selected industries, including automatic access to bank loans for the working capital needed for all export activities. Medium and long term loans for investment are rationed and often available only to firms meeting government export targets and pursuing other requested activities.

14. Reduced public utility taxes and rail rates for exporters.

15. A system of export credit insurance and guarantees, as well as tax incentives for overseas marketing and postshipment export loans by the Korean Export-Import Bank.

16. The creation of free trade zones, industrial parks, and export-oriented infrastructure.

17. The creation of public enterprises to lead the way in establishing a new industry. As Alice Amsden documents, public enterprises produced the first Korean output of ships and refined petroleum products and petrochemicals. Howard Pack and Larry Westphal found that "the share of public enterprises in Korea's non-agricultural output is comparatively high, being similar to India's."

18. Activities of the Korean Traders Association and the Korea Trade Promotion Corporation to promote Korean exports on behalf of Korean firms worldwide.

19. General orchestration of sector-wide efforts to upgrade the average technological level, through use of a new generation of machinery.

20. Government coordination of foreign technology licensing agreements, using national bargaining power to secure the best possible terms for the private sector in utilizing proprietary foreign technology.

21. The setting of export targets for firms (since the early 1960s.) Firms set their own targets, which may be adjusted by the government.

The use of manufacturing exports of growing technological content as a yardstick of performance automatically emphasizes targets with very strong development benefits. In addition, the world export market is an arena in which performance is clearly, quickly, and rigorously tested, while keeping the development ministries, whose resources and information capacities are inherently limited, tightly focused on relevant and manageable problems.

In this regard, export targets as a development policy mechanism hold the distinct advantage over general output targets in that they are easily observable. This fact has long been understood by LDC fiscal authorities which have taxed exports precisely because they are observable and therefore not subject to the tax evasion which is so rampant in the developing world. This distortion has a well-publicized (if not self-evident) anti-export bias effect. South Korea puts this "fiscal observability" to use as the centerpiece of its industrial policy system, in a way which reverses by 180 degrees the negative incentive effects of export taxes.

Enforcement of export targets in the case of Korea is mostly moral or "cultural" in nature, but the evidence seems persuasive that in Korea these have been among the most powerful incentives. South Korea as a whole has an extensive pattern of "rituals" reinforcing these economic incentives with cultural ones. A key ritual in Korean economic life is the Monthly National Trade Promotion Meeting. According to Rhee, Ross-Larson and Pursell,

"Chaired by the president, the monthly trade promotion meetings are select gatherings of the ministers and top bureaucrats responsible for trade and the economy; the chief executives of export associations, research organizations, and educational institutions; and the heads of a few firms, mainly the general trading companies and other large firms. The prominence of those attending shows that the monthly meetings are far more than perfunctory meetings to improve coordination between the private and public sectors."

Firms in the sample were either represented by their particular export association or, in many cases for large firms, represented directly. After briefings, awards are typically presented for excellent export performance. On a more national scale, one of the major national holidays in South Korea is called "Export Day," which has been held on November 30 since 1964, when exports first topped $100 million. As Rhee, Ross-Larson and Pursell describe,

"The focus of the celebration is the award of prizes at a large public gathering, prizes that the heads of firms take seriously. There are President's prizes for being the number one exporter in an industry, for export merit as a small or medium sized firm, for exceeding a target by more than 50 percent. There are Prime Minister's prizes for inventions, for excellence in design, for having a high reputation in exhibitions overseas, or for developing an export product of high quality. And there are prizes for reaching a certain level of exports. There are in addition industry medals and prizes awarded by various ministries. The award of these prizes is akin to the pinning of medals on officers--with salutes, solemnity and sharp strides. The heads of firms typically display the awards in their offices--along with a picture of the president and calligraphy inscribed to the head of the firm and carrying messages on the importance of exporting..."

To what extent is this cultural aspect of the Korean export experience transferrable to other countries? There is no obvious connection between Export Day and Confucianism. The love of public recognition through contests and competitions, medals and prizes seems to be a universal human trait. Recently, such an approach has been adopted successfully by the United States, in the popular Malcolm Baldridge awards. Most likely, the idea could be successfully adopted by other developing countries. In fact, this approach has recently been adopted by Thailand. On the other hand, one may reasonably doubt its effectiveness in the absence of reinforcing economic policies.

Import substitution often precedes, logically and empirically, export promotion.

The influential study of Chenery, Robinson and Syrquin concludes that "periods of significant export expansion are almost always preceded by periods of strong import substitution." Strong support for the implication that this import substitution phase had something to do with the export success that followed comes from the observations that after the switch to export promotion the leading industrial sectors did not change.

In the South Korean case, industrialization began with an import substitution phase in the 1950s and early 1960s. After the country's switch to an export-led growth strategy in the 1960s, selective protection of industry continued to play a very important role in industrial development.

In addition to many domestic content regulations, Richard Luedde-Neurath has described how South Korea maintained a very extensive system of import controls well into the 1980s. What he terms the "Korean Kaleidoscope" includes restrictive trader licensing, widespread quantitative controls, systematic foreign exchange allocation under the Foreign Exchange Demand and Supply Plan, intervention in export-import settlements, required advance deposits (which have been as high as 200% of import value), and capricious customs practices. An important example is that prospective importers must realize minimum export earnings before becoming eligible to import; these obligations began at $10,000 in 1962 and have increased over time to $1,000,000 in 1982.

Pack and Westphal conclude that "through import restrictions, selectively promoted infant industries were often initially granted whatever levels of effective protection were required to secure an adequate market for their output as well as a satisfactory rate of return on investment. Initial rates of effective protection were frequently in excess of 100 percent." The country also utilizes an informal system of indicative planning type protectionist measures. In South Korea, tariffs are primarily collected on final goods and intermediate inputs for domestic sales rather than exports. As Robert Wade notes, tariff rates appear much higher when they are averaged over non-export-related imports only. Finally, Petri presents data that leads him to conclude that Korea has "an unusually protection-prone export bundle."

Thus in the Korean case, import controls may be called a "handmaiden" of successful industrial export promotion. In the first instance, many export industries begin as infant industries requiring protection. Pack and Westphal stress that as a result of the export promotion reforms of the early 1960s, "imports destined (either directly or indirectly as inputs) for the domestic market remained subject to tariffs and quantitative controls.

However, the system of controls on these imports was rationalized and thereby converted from a mechanism of socially unproductive rent seeking into an instrument of industrial promotion." Second, as Luedde-Neurath notes, the developing industrial sector functions as a whole and benefits from externalities and linkages between firms, making a market failure case for general protection. Finally, Alice Amsden has pointed out that in South Korea cross-subsidization across divisions within firms as a company enters new export markets such as shipbuilding is intentionally facilitated by government. Diversified companies understand that they are expected to use the monopoly rents that they earn from these various import barriers as working capital for expansion into new sectors. The state also offers supplemental support for entering new markets as needed.

As Pack and Westphal summarize the evidence, "something approximating neutrality" applies to "established industries... But there has been substantial industry bias in favor of the promoted infant industries."

Given the central role of technological progress in this type of development strategy, it may be asked what role multinational corporations played in transferring technology. There is a large literature exploring the pros and cons of multinational firm presence for development and analysis of policies intended to maximize these benefits and minimize these costs.

A major World Bank study by Westphal, Rhee and Pursell has concluded that "Korea's export industrialization has overwhelmingly and in fundamental respects been directed and controlled by nationals... technology has been acquired from abroad largely through means other than direct foreign investment." The role of multinational corporations in the economy has been much smaller than in most other middle-income countries.

Unquestionably, in the late 1980s and early 1990s, South Korea substantially liberalized. The lesson question is whether they would have done as well had they liberalized sooner. This is a question that can never be answered with certainty. Some economists have argued that South Korea would have industrialized even faster if it had maintained a free trade policy from the beginning. In any case, active industrial policy continues to this day, emphasizing Korean entry into the most leading-edge, high technology fields.

Recently, South Korea's Ministry of Trade and Industry targeted new materials, computer-controlled machine tools, bioengineering, microelectronics, fine chemistry, optics and aircraft as fields in which it predicted that the country could catch up with the US and Japan economically and technologically. Government is involved with the whole process. As South Korea becomes a candidate for developed country status, targeted industrial policies oriented toward technology enhancement are continuing to play a central role. Samsung has already become one of the largest world players in semiconductors.

What stands out in the case of industrial policy in South Korea is the selective involvement of government in projects in which technological progress (product, process or organizational) has been a central concern. This policy theme may be traced from early attempts at achieving technology transfer in relatively basic industries to the current efforts of South Korea to develop original innovative capacity in high technology sectors.

Of course, it is impossible to prove that Korea's industrial policies were responsible for its success. It cannot be ruled out that Korea might have done even better without these policies. But that this is very unlikely is suggested by the fact that the only country to have grown faster over a sustained period in recorded economic history is Taiwan; and that country used a very similar set of industrial policies as did Korea.

But the interpretation which seems most favored by the evidence is that the South Korean industrial policy mix has served to overcome market failures involved in the process of technological progress. That such market failures are endemic to original technological progress is a well-known proposition of economics. But there may have been a massive underestimation of the importance and extent of such market failures in the transfer of product, process and organizational innovations to developing countries.

Obviously, the fact that these policies have been used successfully in South Korea does not automatically negate the arguments that such policies may in general be subject to the corruptions of rent-seeking activities. Understanding how South Korea was successful in this regard while so many others failed will likely be a major focus of development studies in coming years.

As a preliminary conclusion, the case of South Korea suggests that it is a combination of industrial policies addressed to specific market failures, and consistent with underlying market forces (as well as the local political economy) that promotes industrial development. Without proper attention to incentives (for both market and rent-seeking activities), these same industrial policies can prove counter-productive. Countries that cannot find the political will to use protection as a highly selective and strictly temporary instrument of industrial policy in cases where large, identified market failures can be shown to exist, are probably better off abandoning this instrument altogether; the case of Bolivia is probably a good example of this.

In the present period, Korea's now democratic government is making a series of adjustments designed to make its market economy function in a more mature way. In the past, the government encouraged giant conglomerates, or Chaebol, to expand and enter new markets as a way of achieving economies of scale and scope, to facilitate exporting, and to facilitate its control over the economy by keeping the number of companies it had to stay in close contact with small.

Now that the Korean economy is established, the Chaebol are seen as liabilities to further growth. They are also seen as political liabilities, as companies which unfairly received government advantages in the past that other companies did not benefit from. Antitrust regulations are now being enacted and enforced; and this will probably make the Korean economy much more competitive in the future. As the Korean economy approaches maturity, government's role in the productive sector continues to recede.

But the lesson for developing countries that would like to emulate South Korea's success is that until the world technology frontier is approached, government does have an important role, even in the productive sector, until domestically-based private industry can establish itself.

Sources. This case study is largely drawn from Stephen C. Smith, Industrial Policy in Developing Countries: Reconsidering the Real Sources of Export Led Growth, 1991, M.E.Sharpe for Economic Policy Institute, from which financial support is gratefully appreciated. See in addition: Amsden, Alice, Asia's Next Giant: South Korea and Late Industrialization, Oxford: Oxford Univ. Press (1989); Balassa, Bela, "The Lessons of East Asian Development: An Overview," Economic Development and Cultural Change, 36, Supplement, S273-290, 1988; Chenery, Nollis, Sherwin Robinson, and Moses Syrquin, 1986, Industrialization and Growth: A comparative study, New York: Oxford; Dahlman, Carl J., Bruce Ross-Larson and Larry E. Westphal, "Managing Technical Development: Lessons from the Newly Industrializing Countries," World Development, 15, 759-75, 1987;
Frank, Charles R., Foreign Trade Regimes and Economic Development: South Korea, New York: Columbia (for NBER), 1975; Financial Times, May 28, 1993; Keesing, Donald B., The Four Successful Exceptions. Official Export Promotion and Support for Export Marketing in Korea, Hong Kong, Singapore and Taiwan, China, UNDP-World Bank Trade Expansion Program Occasional Paper 2, 1988; Luedde-Neurath, Richard, Import Controls and Export-Oriented Development: A Reassessment of the South Korean Case, Boulder: Westview, 1986; Gordon White, ed., Developmental States in East Asia, New York: St. Martins, 1988; Pack, Howard and Larry Westphal, "Industrial Strategy and Technological Change: Theory versus Reality," Journal of Development Economics, 22, 87-128, 1986
Michael Porter, Competitive Advantage of Nations (NY: Free Press, 1990); Rhee, Yung Whee, Bruce Ross-Larson and Gary Pursell, Korea's Competitive Edge: Managing the Entry into World Markets, Baltimore: Johns Hopkins for the World Bank, 1984; Westphal, Larry E., Yung W. Rhee and Gary Pursell, Korean Industrial Competence: Where it Came From, World Bank Staff Working Paper No. 469, 1981; Westphal, Larry E., Yung W. Rhee, Linsu Kim and Alice Amsden, Exports of Capital Goods and Related Services from the Republic of Korea, World Bank Staff Working Paper 629, 1984; World Bank, Korea: Managing the Industrial Transition (Washington, in 2 volumes, 1987).

15. Guangdong, China: Fastest growth in economic history through exports, direct foreign investment and judicious planning

The larger the productivity gap between countries, the quicker that income can grow once modern economic growth has begun. It seems the gap between traditional and advanced technology can be crossed about as quickly today as a century ago, though the gap between the most advanced and the most backward regions in the world is larger than ever. While Britain doubled its output per person in the first 60 years of its industrial revolution, and America did so in 45 years, Korea accomplished this in the 10 years from 1966-77. Incredibly, Guangdong province in China (adjacent to Hong Kong) recently performed this feat in less than 5 years and is well on its way to doing so again. In 1991, Guangdong grew at an annual rate of 27% and in 1992 at 23%.

Guangdong is the province of China interior to the British colony of Hong Kong and the Portuguese colony of Macao. Between those cities and up the Pearl River lies its capital, Guangzhou, once known in the West as Canton. This Pearl River Delta region is one of the main engines of the recent rapid growth of China, and the driving locomotive for Guangdong, today the wealthiest Chinese province, with a population of about 65 million.

Guangdong benefits from a history of an entrepreneurial culture and exposure to Western business practices dating to the early nineteenth century. The market savvy of the province was never fully extinguished in the command economy period of the mid 1950s to mid 1970s.

Modern Guangdong economic history of rapid development begins in Hong Kong, the British enclave city state surrounded by Guangdong. Hong Kong will revert to Chinese sovereignty in 1997, and has had a long and complex relationship to Guangdong.

Given Guangdong's proximity to Hong Kong, that city became the local symbol of hated capitalism in the Maoist 1950s, 60s, and early 70s. It was relentlessly portrayed in the Chinese media as a center of exploitation and immiserating poverty.

Hong Kong became an industrial center when many industrialists who had previously concentrated in Shanghai moved their factories to Hong Kong after the Communist takeover in 1949. These industrialists benefitted from a continuous flow of migrants leaving the mainland who were willing to work hard for low pay. Hong Kong's niche as a manufacturing center was a departure from its previous function. Before 1949,

Hong Kong had specialized as an "entrepot" (trading and transshipment) center rather than a manufacturing center, for trade between the interior of China and the rest of the world. This role was greatly diminished at the time of the Communist takeover, but the Communists tacitly worked to guarantee Hong Kong's continued viability because of its continued value as a connection--if a covert one--to the outside world.

In a dramatic turnabout, once-despised Hong Kong instead became a symbol of modernity when China reopened to the outside world in the late 1970s. By this time, Hong Kong had become one of Asia's principal centers of industrial know-how and investment capital and one of the famous newly industrialized "four tigers". Hong Kong had benefitted in international commerce from its widespread use of the international language, English. It also gained from the presence of top quality British civil servants transferred there from all over the once sprawling British Empire, who brought good governance. Much more than any other NIC, however, Hong Kong relied on the free market, rather than industrial and trade policies, for its great success.

Technology transfer and direct foreign investment, primarily from Hong Kong or through Hong Kong intermediaries, has unquestionably been the engine of growth for Guangdong. The "demonstration effect," in which the population perceives firsthand relatively high levels of wealth in Hong Kong, at just the time when commitment to Communist values of sacrifice and egalitarianism were waning, should also not be underestimated as a force for entrepreneurial drive, for that elusive human factor in development that David McClelland has called the "need for achievement."

For well over 150 years there has been a migrant flow from Guangdong to Hong Kong, and there have always been many family and personal connections between these territories. This has provided a valuable base on which to build industrial development. Business connections between Guangdong and Hong Kong anticipate the return of Hong Kong to Chinese sovereignty in 1997. This return carries some risks for Guangdong development if Hong Kong declines as a result; but it offers mostly prospective benefits, provided Beijing carries out the reintegration without jeopardizing the continuation of Hong Kong's special commercial advantages.

Guangdong leaders were more oriented toward market reform and ensuring development progress over ideological objectives than those in a majority of the other provinces. From the beginnings of the opening in the 1970s, these leaders became adept at determining what would be permitted by the Communist rulers in Beijing, and in leveraging these specific areas of greater economic freedom to the province's maximum advantage. The most popular local saying revived the ancient Chinese adage that "the mountains are tall and the emperor is far away."

Agricultural reforms stressing more incentives for individual farmers and agricultural markets in place of state distribution were pursued first, and farm output rose dramatically, doubling in the late seventies and early eighties. It does have to be acknowledged that Guangdong benefits from rich delta soil, and its success may not be easily duplicated. Moreover, the growth rate in agriculture probably cannot be sustained. Much of this increase in agricultural output probably represents what economists call a "once-for-all shift," as existing resources are used more efficiently, rather than a large permanent increase in the rate of growth. But the gains have been remarkable despite the caveats.

At the same time, village-owned and collective enterprises were encouraged and grew very rapidly, providing productive employment for farmers no longer needed on the land. Guangdong's leaders then took advantage of special autonomies granted the province in economic matters and of the special economic zone status in three parts of the province, including the dynamic Shenzhen, across the border from Hong Kong's New Territories.

But the leaders also took all other opportunities for pursuing reform that presented themselves. No doubt part of their stance was influenced by their own proximity to Hong Kong as well as the attitudes of their local citizens who could see Hong Kong television. But their attitudes and the favorable climate they created for the private sector has been a factor in Guangdong's success in its own right.

The dynamism and success of the township and collective enterprises represent a unique aspect of the emerging Chinese economy. Whether standing alone or as joint venture partners with foreign firms, these companies have led the growth and export success of the province. Some are really little more than private firms which are employee- or municipality- owned only on paper. But a majority seem to represent a distinctly Chinese form of quasi-public enterprise, which spread the benefits of export success widely to all the employees or town residents, while maintaining incentives for hard work. Information on these township and collective enterprises are hard to come by, but from preliminary indications they will bear close watching in the coming years as a possible model.

One should not underestimate the development damage inflicted by the Cultural Revolution turmoil of 1966-76. On the surface this conflict was ideological in nature, but it reflected in large measure a power struggle over who would succeed Mao after his death. Riots and factional fighting brought with them some damage to industrial machinery and buildings, but the most significant losses of the period were of human capital. Schools failed to function normally for almost a decade. Scholarship of all kinds became politically suspect and discouraged. Work habits flagged and institutions of incentives were sabotaged. If any real ideology prevailed in this period it could be called "anti-incentivism."

Much of the potential accumulation of skills and knowledge lost in the Cultural Revolution period can never be fully recovered, but some progress has been made in training those affected, improving work habits and restoring and upgrading the quality of schools and universities. Unquestionably, part of China's very rapid growth of the past dozen years represents catch-up to lost potential output.

Then the question becomes whether the phenomenal growth of Guangdong, and indeed the impressive growth of China as a whole, represents a once-for-all shift as existing resources are used more efficiently, or represents sustainable growth. In much of China it seems to have been the former, especially in the agricultural sector. But in Guangdong, a permanent higher growth path seems to have been reached in the industrial and service sectors.

Many development scholars have argued that colonies and some other very dependent regions may find their development progress retarded by their dependent status. Modern economic growth, they argue, may be difficult to initiate under these circumstances. Economic history suggests that there are some important insights to be gained from this view. But certainly, the case of Guangdong shows that if the right conditions are met, trade can be a true engine of modern economic growth. Note that China and Guangdong have strong government with significant bargaining power.

Are the phenomenal economic statistics for real? There is a widely held view among foreign businesses involved in Guangdong that if anything, the growth numbers are systematically understated. There is concern about igniting jealousies elsewhere in China and ideological reactions in the Communist Party if Beijing were to realize the amount of profits being made in joint ventures.

But the foreign investment numbers--over $15 billion were said to have been invested through 1992 with about the same level in new commitments--are somewhat exaggerated. Since foreign investment gets special treatment, Guangdong capital is increasingly "laundered" in Hong Kong, after which it reenters Guangdong as "clean" foreign capital. Front companies are known as "false foreign devils." But if anything there is little reason to believe that the total private investment figures are understated.

In 1997, Hong Kong will officially become part of China. Guangdong in the end may become part of a "double-headed tiger" with Hong Kong, rather than a fifth East Asian tiger in its own right. In this scenario Hong Kong would be the regional center for top management and advanced services. But Guangdong also brings much bargaining power to the relationship. The economic consequences for China and the region as a whole bear watching closely.

Sources: Ezra Vogel, One Step Ahead in China, Cambridge: Harvard, 1989; William Byrd, ed.; Stephen C. Smith, Industrial Policy in Developing Countries: Reconsidering the Real Sources of Export Led Growth, 1991, M.E.Sharpe for Economic Policy Institute; Balassa, Bela, "The Lessons of East Asian Development: An Overview," Economic Development and Cultural Change, 36, Supplement, S273-290, 1988; Borus, Michael and Denis Fred Simon, "High Technology in the Pacific Basin: Analysis and Policy Implications," National Academy of Science, 1989; Keesing, Donald B., The Four Successful Exceptions. Official Export Promotion and Support for Export Marketing in Korea, Hong Kong, Singapore and Taiwan, China, UNDP-World Bank Trade Expansion Program Occasional Paper 2, 1988; Gordon White, ed., Developmental States in East Asia, New York: St. Martins, 1988; Washington Post, May 28, 1992. Financial Times, Feb. 22, 1993, Wall Street Journal, Jan. 10, 1992

16. Marketization and Privatization in Chile

The government role in the Chilean economy and society was once one of the most pervasive in the developing world. Beginning with the 1973 military coup, Chile began the longest-running marketization and privatization program in the developing world. Though this program continues, since the 1990 election of President Patricio Aylwin, the government in Chile has moved to chart a middle course, acknowledging an important role for the state in development, but usually outside of productive enterprises. Throughout this history, Chile has moved in fits and starts that epitomize the problems of finding the right balance between market and public regulation. To date, Chile has also had more success with privatization than any other developing country.

In the nineteenth century, state owned enterprises (SOEs) played an important role in Chile's early development, in sectors like the post and telegraph, railroads and ports, and financial services. Like many Latin American economies, SOEs were greatly expanded in number and scope beginning in the late 1930s. Obstacles to international trade and finance brought on by World War II, and to some degree earlier by the Great Depression and its trading blocs, were the proximate motivations. CORFO, a public investment bank and holding company, financed SOE start-ups in oil refining, steel, sugar beet and other sectors. Later, it acquired private firms, usually after they defaulted on CORFO-provided credit.

In 1970, Salvadore Allende, an avowed Marxist, was elected president. While he strongly supported political democracy, he was committed to turning Chile into a fully socialist economy. His most controversial action was the nationalization of copper mining activities, by far the country's most important export industry, and which was largely controlled by foreign interests. Allende took other actions that angered traditional elites, like carrying out rapid, extensive land reform.

Chile had a history of democratic government and a military with a strong commitment to constitutional rule. But with the support of the country's elite, as well as President Nixon in the US, the military joined in with the Latin American trend of that period and overthrew Allende in 1973, killing him and thousands of supporters.

After the 1973 coup, the Chilean government headed by Augusto Pinochet sought successfully to reverse all of the changes of the Allende era. Deregulation, trade liberalization and privatization were the three main components of that reversal. Every market was largely freed from government control with the exception of the labor market, as Alejandro Foxley noted.

Over an 18-year period some 550 firms employing 5 percent of the country's workforce were privatized. Market forces were brought to bear on areas of the economy unknown in other parts of the developing world, including private social security for all but the poorest citizens. Mandatory individual retirement accounts, replacing the former social security system, set the stage for increased savings and an expanded range of financial instruments.

Chile, even under Pinochet, was never really purely laissez-faire. Some hidden subsidies and inducements remained, including a massive government rescue of the financial sector, amounting to 4.6% of GDP from 1982-1986. Many banks which had been privatized in the preceding years had to be renationalized in the 1982 financial crash. In privatization itself, subsidies were offered to the private sector through the sale of assets at little more than half their real asset values. The approximately 50 remaining SOEs in Chile account for some 16% of the country's GDP, a share that is likely to fall primarily as a result of the growth of the private sector. These SOEs are predominantly found in electric power and the important mining sectors.

Fishing companies were privatized in the 1970s but an extensive government role remained, including export market development, technical assistance, and ecosystem regulation. Agriculture is the sector in which the lion's share of new nontraditional exports have been realized, especially in fruits, and lately in wine. There, government has played an active role in targeting potential export sectors, providing infrastructure, developing markets, supporting research, and providing extension services to help realize higher productivity. Today, Chile's exports represent 35% of GNP, and are more diversified than ever before in its history. Chile runs a trade surplus with Japan, its largest trading partner.

This has represented a modest but successful sector policy, and has played an important part in the favorable growth performance of the late 1980s. But it remains unclear if policies for exports of fruit and other specialty farm and forest products centering around larger farms (latifundia and agribusiness) provide a sufficient development strategy in the longer term. Within agriculture, most farms are very small, and most of these seem to have benefitted little, though it is interesting that in the sugarbeet sector, agribusinesses have found it is in their interest to provide small farmers a secure market, a source of credit and technical assistance.

Chile's new democratic government is continuing a broad commitment to market-oriented reforms but is also responding to the apparent need to expand the supporting government role. Thus privatization has an important role to play in most developing countries, but must be understood in context, and does not succeed by simply banishing government from the economic scene.

Privatization in Chile proceeded over several overlapping stages. In 1974-75 360 firms that had been nationalized in the early 70s were returned to their previous owners; most of the rest of these were reprivatized by 1978. This was far easier to carry out than the privatizations of long-term SOEs carried out by Chile in subsequent years (and are more the type that face East Europe in such daunting numbers). Of the 110 enterprises divested in 1975-83, a large share were SOEs formed in the early 1970s Allende regime. Many others were existing private companies in which that government had bought a percentage of the outstanding shares.

From 1978-81, privatization of social services commenced; government officially continued to provide social services only for the poorest groups, and focused on subsidizing demand rather than supply. By 1981, public enterprises represented 24% of GDP, down from 39% in 1973.

Chile experienced rapid growth in the 1976-81 period following three years of severe recession. But this expansion had the earmarks of a speculative bubble, including wild stock speculation. Financial market deregulation took place too quickly and went too far. After the bubble burst in 1982, stocks crashed (falling 36% in 1982 and an additional 33% in 1983), there was a huge wave of bankruptcies including a fifth of all manufacturing companies employing over 50 workers, and unemployment reached 24%. Many of the companies privatized in the 1970s were purchased with a high ratio of debt-to-equity financing. These companies often failed in the recession period, forcing renationalizations in many cases.

In 1983-86, many enterprises "rescued" (nationalized) by Pinochet in the 1982-83 financial crash were reprivatized. Eight of the 15 largest corporations in Chile were privatized in the 1980s. After the Chilean government assumed a large part of the foreign debt in 1983, debt-equity swaps came to play a major role in privatization. Here, considerable use was made of special competitive restrictions, and joint venture arrangements, which reduced fears of exploitation at the hands of multinational corporations with greater financial sophistication and high bargaining power.

The renewed growth of the late 80s had a qualitatively different character, owing to more judicious regulation of the financial system and macroeconomic management. From 1984 through mid-1993, Chile has grown at an average annual rate of over 6.5%, with growth reaching about 10% in 1992. At the same time, inflation fell to 12.7% from

18.7% in 1991. World Bank data show that annual inflation was about 20% for the 1980-1990 period, and about 130% over 1965-1980. Growth rates in the 10% range do create concerns that inflation might be reaccelerated, and growth is expected to fall somewhat in 1993 and 1994. One difference between Chile's recent high growth and previous booms is that growth is investment-led rather than consumption-led.

In 1986-89, and continuing to the present though at a slower pace, at least 27 large industrial enterprises that had been in state hands for a longer time were privatized.

Increasingly, U.S. corporations are producing in Chile not only for the domestic market but for export. Foreign investment continues to flow into Chile in the 1990s, reaching some $1.38 billion by the end of 1992. There is some concern that the rapid inflow will drive up the value of the peso and make exports less competitive, as happened in the late 1970s.

But the country has experienced an apparently permanent drop in the share of manufacturing in GDP, especially in sectors not intensive in their use of local natural resources. This makes its experience to date different from the long-run top performing countries such as Korea and Taiwan; and may pose a challenge if opportunities for productivity gains are concentrated in manufacturing sectors. On the other hand in Chile manufacturing companies were often import substitution industries which were, to say the least, not growing up very fast.

Privatization from the mid-80s on was achieved through public auction, negotiation, sales to pension funds, "popular capitalism" (to small investors) and "labor capitalism" (to employees). Sales of the latter two types represented about 20% of privatization. Finally, even SOEs not slated for privatization were subject to major internal reorganization with the result that efficiency and profitability increased. A World Bank study suggests that efficiency gains have been made, most dramatically the increased sales after the privatization of Chile Telecom. Of course, these actions were taken in the context of an expanding economy. And the World Bank concluded that the largest part of the gains were realized from expanded freedom to hire and fire workers.

"Popular capitalism" was intended to spread ownership among many small individual investors, in part to increase popularity and acceptance of privatization. To become eligible for generous discounts, participants had to be taxpayers with no back taxes owed. Two major banks, Banco de Chile and Banco de Santiago were privatized under this plan.

Under labor capitalism, workers could acquire a percentage of shares in their own companies, up to the value of 50% of a worker's pension fund which could be received in advance for this purpose. Retirement funds could be used as collateral for below-market government loans to buy additional shares. At retirement, workers could elect to trade these shares back for the value of their pension fund, so this provided the workers an essentially riskless investment. About 21,000 workers, 35% of those eligible, took part; other shares were purchased by groups of workers organized as investment societies.

Between 1985 and 1990, 15 SOEs were sold using some employee ownership, including 3 which became 100% employee-owned. Another three became 44, 33, and 31% employee owned, and the remaining nine had an average of about 12% employee ownership. These privatizations have been remarkably successful. Not only have productivity and share values risen substantially, but employment has risen. Employees seem to be working more conscientiously (e.g., taking better care of company equipment) and in some cases firms are allowing workers to use greater judgement on the job.

To date, the conventional wisdom that employee ownership may decrease attractiveness has not been borne out. An example is the National Sugar Industry in Chile, privatized in 1986, in which workers hold a total of 45% of the shares. Despite this, several foreign investors purchased good-sized minority shares, and it is a highly regarded investment. Many U.S.-owned firms are familiar with Employee Stock Ownership Plans and similar programs in the U.S., own countries, and may have introduced ESOPs themselves or seen firms with which they are familiar do so, precisely to improve labor relations and efficiency. Employee stock purchases represent a positive market signal to other potential investors from a group possessing unique insider information. Employee ownership in privatization may also help countries reduce the drastic increases in inequality which often accompany liberalization.

In 20 years of almost constant "structural adjustment" in Chile, the top 10% has gained but the bottom 90% remains worse off. Absolute poverty has also increased: The Inter-American Development Bank reports that the share of families in the Greater Santiago area living in absolute poverty has grown from about one-third to about one-half from the late 1960s to the late 1980s. The sharpest jump occurred in the 1969 to 1976 period, when the percentage of the poor increased from 28.5% to 57%, a historic high. Poor is defined here as having an income less than twice the cost of the "minimum food basket." When we consider only those whose income is even less than the cost of this basket, poverty grew even more dramatically, from 8.4% in 1969 to 22.6% in 1987 (the last year available), after reaching a high of 24.7% in 1986. The poverty rate was also found to be related to the growth rate of the economy, with a two-year lag. A modest increase in resources targeted to the poorest of the poor has also played a role in mitigating absolute poverty.

In the late 80s high growth rates at last were reached--followed by a short slowdown at the start of the 1990s as the economy had become overheated. Poverty and inequality are major concerns of the new democratic government. The new Finance Minister, Alejandro Foxley, was one of the most able critics of the excesses of the ultraorthodox economic policies under Pinochet.

Privatization in Chile has been facilitated by the country's liberal trade and investment rules, and by growing confidence in its macroeconomic stability. Dominique Hachette and Rolf Luders present some empirical evidence that Chilean markets were functioning well enough to provide fair sale prices and to induce efficient operation of privatized enterprises. Other at least mid-income countries that combine fair and objective, or "arms-length," privatization practices with other policies to improve market efficiency should also be able to achieve good results with privatization.

The two largest remaining SOEs are the national copper company, CODELCO, nationalized in 1971, and the National Oil Refinery, ENAP. These are considered very unlikely candidates for future privatization. A 1981 constitutional court ruling prohibited active copper mines from being nationalized. However, the new government has authorized CODELCO to initiate joint ventures with private companies for projects not currently active or unlikely to proceed without co-financing. But certain hydroelectric projects are considered possible candidates for privatization in the near future.

Despite the limitations on devising an optimal plan for privatization and market development, privatization is best not implemented as an isolated part of a development strategy, but as part of a general program for market development. The benefits of privatization will not occur automatically. The role of the state in the economy becomes significantly modified, but is certainly not eliminated.

The supporting institutions of the market will have to grow and develop. Privatization is also easier when SOEs started as nationalizations, especially recent ones, such as the case of Chile's reprivatizations of the 1970s; when markets are already well-developed, when there is strong political will for privatization, and when ordinary employees and citizens perceive themselves to have a positive stake in privatization. The proper balance will vary from country to country and may not be easy to find. Any one country may have to go through years of experimentation before finding the right balance, as the case of Chile exemplifies.

Indicators are at times conflicting and Chile's wild swings of expansion and contraction makes an accurate assessment of long-term trends difficult. But it would appear that Chile today is in an excellent position to move toward a "drive to maturity," in Walt Rostow's phrase. The country began a strong emphasis on education and human development in the 1920s; superior conditions of basic education and health survived the dictatorship period, and Chile enjoys the fruits of this long-term program today.

Despite some errors of excess, for which a price was paid in the form of the financial crash, the modern market institutions that are the foundation of a developed economy were successfully created under the Pinochet regime. One repeated criticism was the "lack of transparency in divestitures," as Dominique Hachette and Rolf Luders put it. As a result, rightly or wrongly, many Chileans came to feel that the process of privatization particularly in its first phase was financially benefitting favored circles and discriminating against ordinary Chileans. This was partly rectified with the "popular capitalism" and "labor capitalism" programs of the late 1980s.

But while undertaken undemocratically and against the will of the majority, the core of these market reforms are now accepted by the majority and will not likely be reversed under democratic rule. One hopes that other countries can follow the constructive features of its example within the democratic process.

At the same time, the new democratic government is wisely giving greater attention to concerns for equity, reversing the cutbacks in social spending of the Pinochet regime by expanding programs in education, basic health care, nutrition, housing, water and sewerage. Tax reform passed in the first year of President Aylwin's government raised $1 billion for social projects and better pay for schoolteachers.

The government is also expanding public investment in other vital infrastructure such as roads, ports and irrigation systems. And it is beginning to diversify the scope of its moderate industrial and export policies to assist development of manufacturing sectors. A first in Latin America, Chile seems to have permanently tamed inflation, projected at about 10% for 1993.
Chile is well-positioned economically and socially in the mid-1990s for successful long-term growth. It has a strongly market-based economy, in which government competently plays an active but targeted role in the areas in which it is most needed.

The country has traveled a rocky road to get there, but today the outlook is very hopeful for Chile's extensively privatized economy, supported where needed by a constructive government role. And while there may be some doubts about the applicability of the experience of Chile to other countries--for example, its is a very modest size country, with a population of only about 13 million--it is an economy that bears watching closely in the coming years.

Sources. This chapter is closely modeled on the comparative case study of Chile and Poland by Stephen C. Smith on Chile and Poland in Michael Todaro, Economic Development, 5th Ed., New York Longman, but provides updated and expanded material. The earlier study provides additional information on employee ownership. Other sources: John Vickers and George Yarrow, "Economic Perspectives on Privatization," Journal of Economic Perspectives, 5, Spring, 111-32 (1991); World Bank, "Techniques of Privatization of State-Owned Enterprises," World Bank Technical Paper 90, in 3 volumes, 1988; S. C. Smith, "Employee Ownership in Privatization in Developing Countries," Ahmad Galal et al, "Welfare Consequences of Selling Public Enterprises, World Bank, 1992; Alejandro Foxley, Latin American Experiments in Neoconservative Economics, Berkeley, U. of Calif., 1984; Inter-American Development Bank, Chile: Socioeconomic Report, Aug. 1991; World Bank, World Development Report 1992; Dominique Hachette and Rolf Luders, Privatization in Chile: An Economic Appraisal, San Francisco: ICS, 1993; Financial Times, Nov. 10, 1992; Chile: A Status Report on Privatization, Business America, May 18, 1992; Wall Street Journal, Jan. 22 and Jan. 25, 1993; The Economist, June 13, 1992; Marco Santamaria, "Privatizing Social Security: The Chilean Case, Columbia Journal of World Business, Spring, 38-51, 1992.

17. Tax Reform in Bolivia

In recent years, many developing countries have undertaken tax reform. From experiences before and after tax reforms, development economists have learned some important things.

First, it does not work to impose tax policy strictly on the basis of Ramsey rules and other staples of conventional optimal taxation theory. (The Ramsey rule is to equalize the "deadweight loss" per unit of tax revenue, to minimize the efficiency cost of taxation.) In developing countries particularly, feasibility and costs of collection of each type of tax proposed must play an important role in the choice of tax instruments. In other words, as Joel Slemrod has put it, we must consider "optimal tax systems" rather than "optimal taxes" in the abstract. Thus the "technology of tax collection" must be considered, which includes the cost of tax administration and enforcement of compliance.

One finding is that "fiscal carrots" seem to work better than "fiscal sticks." Another is that the value added tax, or VAT, may not be the best tax in theory, but it is usually the best tax in LDC practice. It costs less to administer, results in better compliance at least at modest tax rates, is at least not strongly regressive in that large consumers pay proportionately more, and it provides an incentive for saving. More broadly, tax reform is best introduced in conjunction with other trade, macroeconomic and monetary reforms, which should be developed pragmatically and flexibly. Spending reform must proceed in tandem with tax reform. But too extreme an adherence to purely orthodox or to the various "heterodox" alternatives is fraught with danger.

Serious tax reform is exceedingly difficult to implement. It becomes politically feasible only in the most dire economic circumstances. When such windows of opportunity open, they must be used quickly, before they shut. Finally, tax reform is never really complete. Whatever is achieved must be guarded vigilantly. Unfortunately, all tax systems lead to perverse incentives and have other serious drawbacks. All tax systems are compromises across objectives of simplicity, compliance, fairness and, of course, producing adequate government revenue.

One of the most dramatic overhauls of a developing country tax system took place in Bolivia. The Bolivian experience illustrates these tax reform principles.

In the early to mid 1980s, Bolivia was one of the world's basket-case economies. The world recession and the effects of the debt crisis hit Bolivia hard. Official unemployment was over 17%. The government printed money in lieu of collecting taxes and inflation reached a peak annual rate of 24,000% during 1985. Inflation had been 4000% for just the first seven months of that year. The import of Bolivian currency, which was printed abroad, became a significant part of the import bill. Debt servicing consumed a growing portion of export revenues. There was a complete lack of faith in the Bolivian peso, and the US dollar had effectively replaced it as a store of value and unit of account--what is called "currency substitution." Many factors led to this result. A military dictatorship in the 1970s borrowed foreign money promiscuously.

The elected government that followed in the early 1980s was mandated to reduce Bolivia's startling inequality, but was unable to achieve this, and social strife proliferated. Manuel Pastor has argued that the government simply had few degrees of freedom given inflexibility on debt repayment in this period.

The political economy of civil strife led to a total loss of fiscal discipline. In the mid-1980s, the government collected a mere 1% of GNP in taxes, a fiscal policy of "all spending and no taxes." The large budget deficits that followed were the proximate cause of the hyperinflation and economic collapse that followed.

In 1986, the newly elected government of President Victor Paz Estenssoro was able to pass a complete overhaul of the tax system, as well as a wide range of other market liberalization measures. Together these reforms were known as the New Economic Policy. A dramatic tax reform was approved in mid-1986, to become operational one year later. Paz coupled this reform with the toughest balanced budget fiscal policy on record: each day, government would authorize payments of only as much as it was collecting in taxes. The policy was presided over by the tough planning minister, Gonzalo Sanchez de Lozada, one of Bolivia's richest citizens. Bolivia became one of the vanguards of the 1980s marketization movement.

Thanks in large part to tax reform, Bolivia's government budget deficit has been brought under control, and the hyperinflation which derived from it eliminated. Eventually, growth was restored--but at a big upfront cost.

One goal of the Bolivian "tax revolution," as it is called, is to use some parts of the tax system to gain information that may be useful in enforcing other parts of the system. This is a potentially important aspect of designing an optimal "tax system" as a whole.

Most developing countries have a hard time collecting sales taxes (as they do all types of taxes). In the case of sales taxes, individuals and storekeepers often collude, splitting the savings from not paying sales taxes. Taxes are hard to enforce if records of sales are not kept.

Under the Bolivian tax reform, there is now a 10% withholding tax on income from all sources--but this tax can be offset to the extent that individuals furnish proof that they have paid VAT taxes in that amount. This proof is normally in the form of a sales receipt. These receipts can then be used by the new Ministerio de Recaudaciones (Ministry of Tax Collections) to do spot checks on the honesty of retail stores. This is an excellent example of a "fiscal carrot," or positive incentive to play by the tax rules, in distinction from the "fiscal stick" of legal sanctions. Another is the elimination of direct contact between low-level tax officials, who were notoriously easy to bribe in Bolivia under the old system, and taxpayers.

Commercial banks have been enlisted to collect taxes. They get to see the tax returns of their customers, and as an incentive receive 0.8% of taxes they collect. The creation of a new ministry to enforce tax laws acted as a signal to Bolivians that tax avoidance would no longer be taken lightly. Harsh penalties have been introduced for fraud. Most impressively, a tax registration campaign more than doubled the number of officially enrolled business taxpayers (though there is no rigorous evidence that this new registrant information has itself been effectively used to increase compliance).

Tax simplification was an important part of the reforms. Most importantly, individual and corporate income taxes were abolished and replaced with a VAT; companies were to pay a flat 2% tax on net worth (this was later increased to 2.5%). The old system was simply too complex for Bolivia to administer. The income withholding and rebate is used only to ensure compliance with VAT rules. A uniform tariff of 20% was adopted, later reduced to just 10%. The government of Bolivia has become much less dependent on tariffs as a source of revenue. Thus, the incentive for protected firms to produce for the home market rather than for export has been reduced.

Countries that cannot find the political will to use protection as a highly selective and strictly temporary instrument of industrial policy in cases where large, identified market failures can be shown to exist, are probably better off abandoning this instrument altogether, and Bolivia was a good example of this. Further, small taxes whose collection costs were high and were easily flouted were eliminated.

One new measure is a 1% transactions tax. One goal is to collect information that could be useful in other aspects of tax enforcement. This is simple, but causes high rates of tax on sectors which have a very low degree of vertical integration, It also creates incentives for an inefficiently large level of vertical integration mergers, both to avoid the tax and to avoid providing the government with information.

Equity concerns are always an issue in designing a tax system. Equity and efficiency do not always represent tradeoffs in development, as the earlier case study of girls' education demonstrates. Unfortunately, the tax system is one place where we are often presented with a harsh tradeoff. Progressive taxation is fair, and provides taxation with wide political legitimacy. But steeply progressive taxation leads to rampant tax evasion (legal and illegal) by high-income taxpayers, and distorts economic decisions such as where and how much to invest. Complex tax codes encourage tax avoidance and corruption. Lower and flatter marginal tax rates are easier to administer and enforce.

On the other hand very low marginal tax rates for the very rich are politically unsustainable in virtually all countries, as the recent experience in the United States demonstrates. Tax codes biased in favor of the rich may contribute to inequality; and inequality may lead to lower growth. And once issues like tax rates are reopened, so too are the doors for new tax breaks and loopholes for well-connected interest groups; and efficiency gains may prove fleeting.

There is no science of tax rate progressivity. A progressive structure must be chosen that is perceived as fair but is not so steep that it produces large distortions in economic behavior. A tax code must be written that is simple but recognizes that some activities such as equipment investment should be treated differently from other activities such as company perks.

But the case of Bolivia is dramatic. By abolishing the income tax altogether, and replacing it with a VAT, Bolivia is open to the charge of abandoning progressivity altogether (and perhaps creating regressivity). A progressive tax on real estate and vehicles does partially compensate, however. Moreover, Bolivia's previous tax system, while nominally progressive, was flagrantly violated by the rich and the code may have well been significantly regressive in practice.

The question becomes whether nonprogressivity on the revenue (tax) side can be balanced by progressivity on the expenditure side. That is, if the government spends more money proportionately on important services for the poor, such as agricultural extension, basic education, prenatal and infant nutrition, and so on. Even so, it remains to be seen if the lack of an income tax for the very rich is politically sustainable in Bolivia. Widespread complaints, which come down to arguments that the tax system is not progressive enough, can be heard voiced throughout the country.

Major efforts have been made to reduce corruption by more honest parts of the bureaucracy, such as the Comptroller-General's office, which is armed with tough new auditing powers. But forces of corruption, including resurgent power of drug traffickers, are proving tenacious in Bolivia as in much of Latin America.

Certainly Bolivia's tax and broader market reforms have achieved some important successes. Inflation was only 9% in 1992, lowest in Latin America. In 1993, Sanchez de Lozada was elected president in a free election, which shows that making politically daring decisions like implementing tax increases and cutting wasteful government spending does not have to mean political suicide. If it ultimately brings an overall improvement for most voters, they will forgive their loss of specific benefits--at least if politicians are also astute at making grand political gestures, like naming a native Bolivian as his vice-presidential running mate, as Sanchez de Lozada did in Victor Hugo Cardenas. Sanchez de Lozada has ambitious growth targets and a "popular capitalism" privatization plans which would distribute substantial proceeds to the Bolivian people.

By 1990, the government was collecting 14% of GNP in taxes, up from 1% five years earlier. GDP growth has been positive but modest: 2.2% in 1987, 2.8% in 1988, and 2.5% in 1989. But with population growth close to 3%, real GNP per capita was still declining several years into the program. The World Bank has described Bolivian poverty as at "Sub-Saharan levels." The main exports are still tin, natural gas and, despite efforts to eradicate it, cocaine. Balance of payments problems have not been successfully resolved.

The promise of restored growth of the Bolivian "tax revolution" and related market reforms has yet to be fully realized. After more than seven years, the jury is still out on Bolivian tax reform and the wider political and economic transformation of which it is a part.

Sources. Arthur P. Mann, "Bolivia: Tax Reform 1986-89," Bulletin for International Fiscal Documentation, 44, 32-35, 1990; Joel Slemrod, "Optimal Taxation and Optimal Tax Systems," Journal of Economic Perspectives, 4, 157-78, Winter 1990; Newbery, David and Nicholas H. Stern, eds., The Theory of Taxation for Developing Countries, NY: Oxford (1987); Javid Khalilzadeh and Anwar Shah, eds., "A Symposium on Tax Policy in Developing Countries," in the World Bank Economic Review, 5, 3, pp. 459-573, Sept. 1991; Richard M. Bird, "Tax Reform in Latin America: A Review of Some Recent Experiences," Latin American Research Review, 7-36; World Bank, Bolivia; Richard Musgrave Fiscal Reform in Bolivia, Harvard Law School, 1981; Malcolm Gillis et al, eds., Tax Reform in Developing Countries, Durham: Duke, 1989; Manuel Pastor, Inflation, Stabilization and Debt: Macroeconomic Experients in Peru and Bolivia, Boulder: Westview, 1992; Diego Abente, "The Political Economy of Tax Reform in Venezuela," Comparative Politics, 199-216, Jan. 1990; Ramiro Cabezas, "Bolivia's Tax Reform of 1986," Tax Notes International, 2, 529-39, 1990; Financial Times, various issues; The Economist, various issues, 1985 and 1986.

18. AIDS: Economic Development Impact and the Case of Uganda

The AIDS epidemic is spreading fast in the Third World, threatening to halt or even reverse years of hard-won human and economic development progress in numerous countries. Though usually thought of as an issue of health care systems and delivery, AIDS is equally an issue of Third World economic development.

AIDS, the final and fatal stage of infection with HIV, the human immunodeficiency virus, is still widely perceived in the Third World as a disease of developed countries and one primarily afflicting homosexuals. In fact, these perceptions are far from reality. The World Health Organization (WHO) estimates that by 1992, over 10 million people worldwide were infected with HIV, with well over 8 million of these, including over one million children, in LDCs. So far, the center of the epidemic has been in tropical Africa, where cases of HIV infection are estimated to have tripled from 2 million to 6 million cases from 1988 to 1992; may pass 10 million by the end of 1994; but will reach a peak rate of new infections of just under 1 million per year between 1992 and 1994.

The next epicenter will be Asia, where the WHO projects new annual cases are approaching 1 million per year, but will not peak and level off until 2010. The WHO's estimates that 30-40 million will be infected worldwide in 2000 are considered conservative by some researchers, and alternative estimates have gone as high as 120 million. More conservative computer models project up to seventy million infections by 2015.

Haiti, the Dominican Republic, Brazil and Mexico are also seriously affected, and homosexual and bisexual men are still the highest risk group in Latin America. But in the developing countries as a whole AIDS is primarily transmitted by heterosexual intercourse; infected blood and drug needles, both by drug abusers and in hospitals, and perinatal transmission (from mother to fetus) also play significant roles. There can be a very long incubation period but average survival once AIDS symptoms set in is under one year in LDCs. Death from AIDS comes much more quickly in Third World than in developed countries. AZT and other expensive treatments are not available to over 99% of the infected. Treatments are generally limited to aspirin, antibiotics for infections, and cortisone for skin rashes.

The problem of AIDS for development is an inherently multidisciplinary problem, involving not just medicine and medical research, but economics and most of the social and behavioral sciences. Sociologists or anthropologists must determine who the prime infection-spreading groups are in various regions, what is most risky about their behavior, and how to effectively change that behavior. Simulation models may also be useful in designing strategy. These models suggest that more significant reductions in the spread of HIV can be realized through changes in sexual behavior than through needle sterilization efforts.

In most cases, in order to halt the spread of HIV, sexual behavior must change. Unfortunately, sexual behavior is far harder to change than medical procedures. A spokesperson for an advertising agency volunteering services for an AIDS awareness campaign in Thailand called attention to the resources that go into persuading people to change simple behaviors like favored brands of soap, a smaller problem than changing sexual behavior which is more basic and ingrained. Persuasion among less educated people prone to superstitious beliefs is all the more difficult.

Here is a look at six of the most important development issues raised by AIDS.

1. Population growth. AIDS could noticeably reduce the rate of population growth in the most affected countries, up to one percentage point per year by some estimates. But even under the worst credible scenarios, nowhere is population expected to decline outright. The occasionally expressed idea that AIDS will reduce the importance of family planning as a top development priority is muddled and irresponsible. The population pyramid is unlikely to change noticeably, since children increasingly are as affected as adults. We can only speculate at this time what the effect of AIDS might be on family fertility choice. On the one hand, women who discover they are infected may stop bearing children. Relatives caring for orphaned children may reduce their own fertility rates. On the other hand, there is evidence that some infected women might decide to have more children while they remain alive, despite the 30% or higher chance the baby would be born infected. Sexual behavior change and a wish to ensure that one does not marry an infected partner might lead to a lowered age of marriage, which could increase total fertility. In Uganda the projections for population growth are for a reduction of growth of up to half a percent per year, which would still leave population growth at an extremely high level of 2.6%.

2. Basic needs. The grim fact is that AIDS is creating a virtual generation of orphans in some African countries such as Uganda. When economically active adults die of AIDS they leave behind dependents including children and seniors who become more vulnerable to absolute poverty. Over one million AIDS orphans have been projected for Uganda and at least ten million Africa-wide by 2000. The World Bank has estimated that in East Africa, each woman dying of AIDS leaves three children orphaned. Providing

basic needs for these orphans, ensuring that they are not discriminated against out of irrational fears, and are able to obtain the few years of schooling that will help rescue them from absolute poverty will be a major development challenge. It is not a challenge that Africa, with all its problems, is accustomed to. Extended family networks have served to provide privately for children who have lost their parents. In some parts of East Africa this traditional family adaptation to death appears on the verge of collapse because of the scope of the AIDS crisis. In Uganda the response to the orphan problem is to try to keep rural children on their farms so they can later support themselves; and otherwise to place children with relatives even if they are not immediate family. The policy to keep orphans living on their farmland is productive in some ways but serious problems remain. These children are often in need of counseling and social workers carry staggering caseloads. Orphaned teenage girls living alone on their farmland are sometimes preyed upon by thieves--and rapists who may carry HIV.

3. Urban modern sector investment and development. Modern sector enlargement is dependent on savings. AIDS is likely to lead to national dissavings as earnings fall and the sick have to be cared for. This may be partly balanced by foreign savings. Aid may increase; on the other hand direct foreign investment may very well decrease. In Uganda there has been considerable new support because of the very severe AIDS epidemic there. Many other countries will soon have an AIDS epidemic of the magnitude of Uganda's, and resources will be diverted to those regions. Companies attracted to cheap and plentiful labor may reconsider their choice of a host country so long as they anticipate lowered supply and higher cost of labor as a result of the AIDS epidemic.

4. Migration and the urban informal sector. There is growing evidence that the spread of HIV is strongly facilitated by active movements of migrant labor. Migrants, especially young males, are more likely to adopt high-risk behaviors including frequent visits to prostitutes and intravenous drug use. They may bring HIV infection with them when they visit their home village.

5. Rural/ agricultural sector development. Uganda has one of the world's highest percentages of the labor force engaged in farmwork, some 86%. A decrease in labor supply may mean a threat to "food security," or it may lead to a switch in crop composition away from labor-intensive agriculture. This may mean a switch away from cash crops and reduce foreign exchange earnings.

6. Education and Human capital. AIDS predominantly strikes young adults in their most productive years. Although infectious childhood diseases still kill far more people in developing countries, AIDS strikes those who have successfully run this

gauntlet of child killers. Throughout Sub-Saharan Africa AIDS is well on its way to becoming the leading cause of death of adult males in economically active years (15 to 49). Urban areas have been hit first, but the virus is rapidly spreading into rural areas. Their societies are counting on the energies and skills of precisely the part of the population most afflicted. Labor shortages in specific skill categories are already emerging in Africa and will get worse.

Estimates of the net impact of AIDS on GNP would be highly speculative. A computer simulation model of Cameroon, designed to mirror the way its market economy works (a computable general equilibrium model), has confirmed the projection that the economic impact of AIDS is vastly magnified if the highly skilled are most affected. A macro model for Thailand indicated that the economic losses due to AIDS deaths is far greater than that due to increased medical care costs. But extensive reliance on standard multisector macroeconomic models for dependable numbers is very hazardous for the case of AIDS impact, because such models assume that the structure of the economy remains the same after a shock; whereas a brutal AIDS epidemic may lead to a collapse of the socio-economic system as it had existed. Beyond this, GNP counts market activity, whereas the impact of uncounted economic activity of women on the farm and in the household may be large and spill over into the market sectors.

Since AIDS raises not just health issues, but development issues as well, an effective AIDS response must involve all the major development agencies and national ministries. WHO has taken the lead with its Global Program on AIDS, or GPA--much weightier than the GPA most students are accustomed to worrying about. Most development agencies are coordinating AIDS efforts with WHO.

The case of Uganda has received considerable attention. Other African countries almost certainly have a higher rate of infection than Uganda, already a numbingly high 10% of the whole Ugandan population according to the WHO. Infection is unevenly distributed demographically and geographically; in Rakai District, for example, over 40% of men and women between 20 and 30 years of age are HIV positive. Some 20% are infected in the capital, Kampala.

A UNICEF study found that by 1989 there were already 600,000 orphans in Uganda, at least double the number of orphans there would be without AIDS, even given the effects of civil war and other widespread diseases. In hard-hit Rakai district, more than one in eight children are orphans, two-thirds of these because of AIDS.

Uganda illustrates the fact that the course of the disease can not be separated from the socioeconomic context in which it propagates. Uganda has a history of disastrous development decisions, and reversing some of these would mitigate the development impact of the AIDS crisis. In 1972, the unbalanced dictator Idi Amin expelled a majority of South Asian entrepreneurs from the country and confiscated their property. Asians then formed the nucleus of commercial agriculture and commerce in Uganda. (The effects on one Ugandan Asian family is a subject of the celebrated movie, "Mississippi Massala.") The economy suffered severe hardships following these expulsions and other perverse economic policy decisions, some of which led indirectly to the AIDS epidemic.

Commercial controls led to an extremely active smuggling industry. Illegal, highly paid truck smugglers, often stranded for days in towns along smuggling routes, made frequent use of prostitutes, encouraging the rapid spread of the disease. At the same time, the harshly dependent status of women, with widespread polygyny and generally weak foundations of marriage as an institution led to high rates of divorce, prostitution, and other types of rapid sexual partner changes.

Women's effective inability to own land despite the fact that they do most of the farmwork creates incentives for both sexes that anthropologists claim leads to this pattern of rapid sexual partner changes, that is so conducive to the spread of HIV, while reinforcing low and declining agricultural productivity. There is little doubt that the horrendous conditions of rural women in Uganda, and Africa in general, is a crucial root cause of the rapid spread of HIV there.

The government of Uganda, a largely Catholic country, long resisted the promotion of condom use and was slow even to acknowledge the widespread presence of the disease. But after this slow start, the Ugandan government now has one of the most active and comprehensive AIDS prevention programs in Africa. Programs are coordinated by the new Ugandan AIDS Commission Secretariat. The Commission is charged with "policy formulation and setting of priorities as well as overseeing, coordinating and facilitating all AIDS prevention, control and management activities throughout the country." Funding has been provided by UNICEF, WHO, USAID, the World Bank and the UNDP. Donor countries including the United States are probably more active on AIDS in Uganda than other countries as a result of the extensive attention to the problem there.

The Ugandan government is now making it easier for Ugandan Asians to reclaim their property, despite resistance from Ugandans who have profited from it. Even the relatively few number of successful returnees to date are making a positive difference, reinvesting in their now dilapidated factories. Effects of saner economic policies would help compensate for losses due to AIDS.

As is so often the case in development, private voluntary organizations (PVOs) are playing the leading role in developing creative, effective responses at the grassroots level. The Ugandan PVO, The AIDS Support Organization (TASO) has played a crucial role in treatment, family assistance, and counseling. Mass media was used, sometimes to good effect, but unpretested commercials have sometimes been misinterpreted or have even backfired. A famous example was the slogan "zero grazing," which was a locally sophisticated way of saying "stay with one partner," but which many ordinary people did not understand.

Condom use has increased in Uganda and some other African countries, but is still very limited. In particular there is extremely little acceptance of condom use among married or regular partners, regardless of the amount of extramarital sexual activity. But the AIDS film, "It's Not Easy," was a great success that was viewed by some 90% of Uganda's workforce. Together, these public and private efforts do have a real effect. Tee-shirts are to be seen everywhere with mottos like "Love Carefully." In Uganda the prostitution industry in towns known to be highly infected has dropped dramatically.

But Tony Barnett and Piers Blaikie's report on studies of AIDS in Uganda shows how far there still is to go. It is widely believed among Ugandans that people who discover they have AIDS deliberately infect others sexually. There is at least some evidence that this actually happens there, as men with the disease have admitted trying to infect women, including through rape. This is reportedly motivated by anger at having to "die alone." Women infected with HIV are reported to take a gamble at bearing children so they do not "feel cheated by death." If ghastly attitudes like these are indeed commonplace, it will be a formidable task to get the epidemic under control, whatever economic incentives and social programs are put in place.

The spread of HIV has been demonstrated to be significantly promoted by the presence of other sexually transmitted diseases (STDs). In both Asia and Africa, transmission of HIV is abetted by widespread prostitution, especially in conjunction with other STDs whose sores promote viral invasion, and by poor hospital hygiene due in part to resource shortages. Other core transmitters of the virus have included truck drivers and military personnel. The cost effectiveness of AIDS education campaigns can be highest when aimed at high-risk groups who start with a low rate of HIV infection. A useful rule of thumb for targeting regions and subpopulations is to find groups who combine low HIV infection rates with high incidence of other STDs.

Though the AIDS epidemic has spread most quickly in Africa, the evidence is that Asia will soon surpass it in numbers of new cases and then total cases. Much of the attention in Asia has centered on Thailand, where newly affluent modern sector workers are said to commonly visit prostitutes almost daily and prostitution is packaged as "sex tours" for foreign businessmen. 600,000 people, over one percent of the Thai population, are already estimated to be infected, and at the current rate of dissemination the figure will reach 10% within 10 years. Slowing an effective response is the fact that AIDS has been widely viewed by Asians as a "foreigner's disease."

Thailand may have the highest infection rate today in Asia. But other Asian countries are not far behind. In India, over 1 million people are already estimated to be HIV positive, but over 95% of the blood supply there is not being tested for the virus. Indonesia has not been seriously affected yet, but is estimated to have close to one million prostitutes. Malaysia has about one million intravenous drug users.

In sum, as the case of Uganda reveals, each sector of the developing economy, and indeed every aspect of human development will be severely, if sometimes indirectly, affected by an AIDS epidemic. AIDS is much more than a health issue, and all agencies concerned with development must work with health officials to halt its spread. The later the development of an effective AIDS policy, the greater the ultimate costs such as medical care, undereducation of orphans, and output loss. These costs cannot be estimated accurately but the magnitudes are so large that even a high discount rate does not alter the conclusion that early intervention is urgent.

An effective response to the problems of AIDS and development will require a careful balancing act of policy making. Despite the human tragedy and development catastrophe of the AIDS epidemic, it is important not to let resources for HIV programs overshadow other worthwhile development projects. At the same time, the potential problem is severe enough that development project planners need to keep the problem at the forefront of attention. Each new health, population and basic needs project is now required by several development agencies to either contain an HIV component or to justify why this is not relevant or cost-effective for the project. This requirement is likely to adopted by virtually all development agencies in the near future.

Sources. Population and Development, Jan. 1993, Special Issue on "A Cultural Perspective on HIV Transmission," Jill Armstrong, "Socioeconomic Implications of AIDS in Developing Countries," Finance and Development, Dec. 1991; "The Unfolding AIDS Disaster in Asia," Business Week, Feb. 22, 1993; HIV and Development, a UNDP packet, especially Desmond Cohen, The Economic Impact of HIV; New York Times, March 22 and March 23, 1993; Financial Times, April 7, 1993; Jean-Louis Lamboray and A. Edward Elmendorf, Combatting AIDS and other Sexually Transmitted Diseases in Africa World Bank Africa Technical Department Paper 181; Lewis, Maureen A., et al, AIDS in Developing Countries: Cost Issues and Policy Tradeoffs, Washington: Urban Inst. 1989; Kambou, Devarajan and Over, CGE Model of AIDS in Cameroon, World Bank, 1991; Myers et al, Macro Model of AIDS in Thailand, 1991; Tony Barnett and Piers Blaikie, AIDS in Africa: Its Present and Future Impact, NY: Guilford, 1992; Jonathan M. Mann, et al, eds., AIDS in the World, Cambridge: Harvard, 1992.

19. Countertrade in Indonesia

Countertrade, or "reciprocal" trade agreements involve payment in goods instead of currency. More precisely, countertrade is a contractual arrangement which links the export of a good to the import of other goods. This can be as simple as straight barter agreements, which is the oldest form of trade.

But the most common type of countertrade agreement, called counterpurchase, involves two linked contracts to purchase goods, usually manufactured goods from developed countries and basic commodities from LDCs. The commodities are to be delivered later at the contractual price. This acts like a no-interest loan to the LDC for the length of time until delivery. The import agreement is transferable to a third party. In addition there are offsets, in which exporters are required to purchase or assemble components locally; buy-back agreements, in which an exporter of factories or equipment agrees to buy back a given quantity of goods manufactured with these capital goods; and production sharing, in which a percentage of output rather than a fixed quantity of output is repurchased.

No one knows how much of world commerce involves some form of countertrade, because there are no reporting requirements, and few formal rules, as agreements in many countries are often arranged separately on a somewhat ad hoc basis. Many countries would rather not emphasize their countertrade activities, because almost by definition this would mean an admission that the country has payments problems. Estimates have ranged from 8% to as high as one third.

These various forms of countertrade will be clarified with some examples in the case of Indonesia. Counterpurchase can be seen in the agreement by Mitsui of Japan to import Indonesian shrimp, cacao beans, frog legs, yellow corn, Kapk oil, plywood, and reinforced rods in exchange for about $8 million worth of machine tools. Barter countertrade can be seen in an agreement with in which Iran will supply $300 million in crude oil to be refined in Java, in exchange for rubber, paper products and tea. Buy-back countertrade can be seen in the agreement by Shell Overseas Investment of the Netherlands to build a petrochemical complex in central Java and accept payment in some $150 million worth of petrochemical products. Finally, offset can be seen in an agreement valued at $337 million with General Dynamics to purchase F-16 aircraft provided that an Indonesian company, PT Nusantara, is subcontracted by General Dynamics to produce aircraft component parts. Various forms of countertrade are most commonly seen in military procurement.

The US has generally discouraged countertrade, but its Agriculture and Defense departments, along with farm state senators, have been interested in countertrade of surplus US foodstuffs for strategic raw materials.

At first appearance, countertrade is a step backwards for the efficiency of the international trading system, and the International Monetary Fund has strongly discouraged the practice. It appears to be a return to bilateralism, which requires that each agent have balanced trade with each other trader over time, rather than more advanced multilateralism, in which trade must be balanced over time with all countries rather than with each country. Put more dramatically, it seems to be a reversion to a primitive form of barter, which relies on the "coincidence of exchange." Other drawbacks: firms become involved in sectors in which they have no marketing or other expertise, or choose to produce in a country that would otherwise be an uneconomical choice.

As with many other issues in economics, simple rules like 'multilateralism is always more efficient than bilateralism' prove too simple to be completely general once problems of imperfect information, risk aversion and externalities are factored into the analysis. With this broadened perspective, countertrade has at least four potential advantages for developing countries, but these carry risks as well.

First, it acts like a forward market when these are otherwise unavailable. The LDC sells a commodity in a future date at a price determined today. This helps the LDC smooth export earnings fluctuations. Of course, this does not mean countertrade is a better alternative over creating such forward markets.

Second, when repayment is in commodities to be delivered later, costs of borrowing may actually be lowered. Commodity IOUs may be more secure than local currency, which may lose value quickly, and more certain to be available than foreign exchange, which has to be earned, and for which other creditors may claim precedence. These IOUs may sometimes even be traded from company to company, and so represent a form of commodity-backed money. Of course, this is not a superior alternative to getting the government's external debt under control, and its fiscal and monetary affairs in order, so that countertrade isn't needed to play this role.

Third, countertrade can be an aid for LDC export promotion. It can offer a strategy for at least initially opening up new export markets. Buy-back and production sharing can offer a strategy for implementing industrial policy. But when strictly required as a condition for business, countertrade policy can backfire. Costs of exporting are likely to be increased, since either firms must become involved in exporting commodities in which they have no experience, or they must pay brokers' fees to those who do have this experience. Finally, as an industrial policy strategy, this will be effective only if the government has correctly picked an "infant" industry. Otherwise, the policy will impose opportunity costs including government subsidies that might have been used for other purposes.

It is sometimes said, "no countertrade--no trade at all," and though this is generally an exaggeration, this saying reflects the fact that countries with debt service difficulties or other payments problems may have difficulty getting trade credits. Under these circumstances the three factors just noted become important.

Indonesia illustrates well both the potential merit and the common pitfalls of countertrade.

In 1981, the government of Indonesia promulgated a new regulation that as a condition of being awarded construction or procurement contracts, foreign contractors would be required to successfully export an equal value of Indonesian commodities, or purchase them themselves. These exports were to be above what the contractor would normally purchase or would normally be sold otherwise. The regulation would apply to all contracts worth 500 million rupiah, or about $450,000. One of the expressed purposes of the law was to diversify its exports. The commodities had to be from among 33 products on an officially approved list, that included rubber, tin, coffee, spices, fish, and plywood.

Interestingly, Malaysia introduced its countertrade laws in direct reaction to the Indonesia law. Malaysia was concerned that Indonesia would "chisel" into its oil, rubber and tin market share. According to Kenton Elderkin and Warren Nordquist, this kind of "domino effect" in mandated countertrade has been common around the developing world.

Today, Indonesia no longer mandates countertrade. Malaysia has since removed basic commodities, which comprise the bulk of its exports, from its countertrade list. Results of the requirement for Indonesia were mixed at best. Some contractors refused to bid under these restrictions. Others insisted on detailed negotiations which sometimes led to delays in exports rather than expediting them. Indonesia concluded that the countertrade restrictions were causing it to lose cash sales. Once countertrade exports left the country, Indonesia could not control the chain of trading in these commodities, but the country discovered that end purchasers were often their regular cash customers, who then imported less from Indonesia on a direct cash basis. Because of such fungibility, growth of countertrade is likely to be limited.

In the future the main role for countertrade will likely continue to be in military procurement, in new export sectors and as a means of carrying out targeted industrial policy. Offsets, including in the military sector, are likely to become a larger share of total countertrade. They are often seen when credit-worthy developing countries are in a strong bargaining position to purchase manufactured goods for which there is excess capacity and for which price discrimination in these LDCs' favor can be possible. While countertrade may be expected to grow, it will probably no longer grow faster than world trade as a whole.

Sources: Mark Casson and Francis Chukujama, "Countertrade: Theory and Evidence," in P.J. Buckley and J. Clegg, Multinational Enterprises in Less Developed Countries, New York: St. Martins, 1988; Bruce Fitzgerald, "Countertrade Reconsidered," Finance and Development, June 1987; The Banker, v. 136, April 1986, p.52; Aspy P. Palia, "Countertrade Practices in Indonesia," Industrial Marketing Management, 21, 273-279, 1992; Kenton Elderkin and Warren Nordquist, Creative Countertrade: A Guide to Doing Business Worldwide, Cambridge: Ballinger, 1987

20. Innovation in Rural Development or Land Reform in Reverse? Opening the Ejidal Sector to Private Investment in Mexico

Amy Grat Contributed Substantially to this Case Study

Latin America is well-known for its inordinately unequal agrarian system, in which large, paternalistic, often inefficient Latifundia exist side-by-side with tiny, labor-intensive, impoverished minifundia. Numerous studies have demonstrated that a system of family size farms or medium corporate or cooperative farms are more efficient than the latifundia-minifundia system.

In Latin America, Mexico was one of the few countries to take great strides toward land reform. Land redistribution is a central legacy of the Mexican Revolution of 1910-1917, and is deeply etched into the Mexican consciousness. The 1917 Mexican Constitution instituted the process of land reform and sanctified the *ejido*, or commons, as a preferred form of peasant land tenure. Since then, more than one-half of Mexico's total land and roughly two-thirds of its cropland have been redistributed from larger estates to small farmers under the *ejido* system.

But Mexico illustrates that the kind of land reform and the support given for small farmers can be just as important as the act of land reform itself. The *ejido* system was inefficiently designed, with overregulation providing poor incentives for farmers, while necessary support in training and credit facilities was lacking. The cumulative effects on economic performance were very adverse.

In Mexico, the agricultural sector contains one-fourth of the labor force and one-third of the population, yet it represents less than 8% of national income. In terms of poverty alleviation, the agricultural sector is a critical arena for action: like many LDCs, some 70% of Mexico's poor are in rural areas.

In November 1991, Mexican President Carlos Salinas de Gotari declared his administration's intention to amend Article 27 of the Constitution so as to end the redistribution of land and to open the way for the "profound transformation" of the *ejidal* sector that would "sow a new seed of freedom and autonomy in the rural areas." The resulting legislation aimed to open up the land reform or *ejidal* sector to private investment. In December 1992 the legislation was overwhelmingly approved by the Chamber of Deputies.

The *ejidal* sector comprises 28,058 *ejido*s on 250 million acres, employing 3.1 million *ejidatarios*, and helping provide for some 12 million of their dependents. The peak of land redistribution occurred under the Cardenas administration (1934-40) with 17,906,429 hectares given in land grants (9.1% of Mexico's surface). By the 1960s, the best croplands had been distributed, and under the de la Madrid administration (1982-88), land redistribution was declared ended. As a result of this program, Mexico's land distribution has become one of the most equal in Latin America, though still much more unequal than that of successful East Asian countries such as South Korea and Taiwan.

An *ejido* consists of twenty or more *campesinos*, or peasants, eligible for land grants. Under the previous Agrarian Reform Law, all members of an *ejido* must work the land personally. Land was not to be privately owned, but to belong ultimately to the nation. The ejidatario farmer was given usage rights, but could not sell, mortgage, sharecrop, or rent the property. *Ejidal* parcels could only be passed on intact to a single heir. In addition to usage rights over individual parcels, *ejidatarios* had access to communal grazing and forestry lands.

Although land redistribution covered 54% of the total national territory in 1988, only 12-13% of that land was under production during 1989. It is estimated that the maximum feasible area for crops is not more than 18% of the total land area. The lack of productivity in the *ejidos* is seen as a constraint on additional growth.

Within the *ejidal* sector the levels of input use and technical efficiency are considered particularly low. According to 1988 *ejidal* census figures, only 17% of all arable *ejido* land was irrigated. 62.2% of all *ejidos* had no agricultural installations such as stables, silos, livestock dips, or hatcheries. 42% had no tractors. 89.3% operate without agricultural equipment such as sawmills, dehydrating plants, and packaging plants. There is also a gap in public services, with 31.7% communities without electric lights, 51.9% without piped potable water, and 78.2% without paved roads.

Part of the reason for this low productivity has been in part due to the paternal input and credit relationship between the government "parastatal" enterprises such as Productora Nacional de Semillas (PRONASE) and Banco Nacional de Credito Rural (BANRURAL) and the *ejidal* sector. Without the ability to use their lands as collateral, *ejidos* have been reliant on government for sources of credit. Up until 1990, inputs had been provided in kind by BANRURAL, rather than allowing farmers to control their own purchases. Decisions about crop mixes and usage of inputs were instituted in a top-down fashion, by extending credit based on government subsidy policies. The result has been that *ejidatarios* have not responded to price changes quickly. Additionally, insufficient or late deliveries of inputs such as fertilizer or seed, and widespread corruption have led to inefficient allocation of resources.

Less than 1% of the total foreign investment flowing into Mexico in 1991 went to agriculture. For some reason the use of development banks such as Grameen in Bangladesh have not been seriously considered.

Another economic rationale for a change in agrarian policy is the required opening of the agricultural sector under the North American Free Trade Agreement (NAFTA). This has resulted in the gradual elimination of government subsidies for fertilizer and seeds. It is the driving force behind a change in the national food policy from one of "self-sufficiency" (represented by the program Sistema Alimentario Mexicano) to one of "food security" based on specializing according to comparative advantage.

Recent negotiations of NAFTA have resulted in an agreement to eliminate corn subsidies over the next 15 years. Since two-thirds of all *ejidatarios* grow heavily subsidized corn, 90% under arid or semi-arid conditions, and produce at yield rates far below the U.S. average, it will benefit the government to reduce the number of people in that sector and move them into "crops more suitable to Mexico's terrain and market position." The opening up of the *ejidal* sector is part of a government plan to reduce by two-thirds the number of farmers who plant corn by 1996.

Additionally, the *ejidos* system has been criticized as impeding new investment on the part of private landholders, due to fears of expropriation. The new law allows private landholdings to be improved through capital investments (such as irrigation) without being "reclassified" for redistribution.

Finally, there is the perceived need to legitimize what is already occurring in many parts of Mexico. Estimates for scope of "illegal" leasing of *ejidal* lands range from a rate of 35%-50% in the Bajio to 50%-90% in the irrigated districts of Sonora and Sinaloa. By bringing these arrangements into the open, better legal protection can be extended to both *ejidatarios* and private investors.

Tenure insecurity, the fear that peasants may lose title or the right to use their land, is a chronic problem, both in the *ejidal* sector and among large private landholders. Due to minimum holding size requirements for *ejido* registration and to the lack of a thorough survey, many *ejidatarios* are without usufruct titles.

Although earlier law permits *ejidos* to be farmed both individually and collectively, the vast majority of *ejidos* are "parceled," where each household is allocated its own tract of land and keeps the income that is generated. Collectively-farmed *ejidos* comprise only 3% of all *ejido* lands. The usufruct nature of the *ejidal* system has not kept the process of *minifundismo*, or subdivision into very small parcels, from occurring. The average parcel size in the *ejidal* sector is just 7.3 hectares, despite the 10 hectare prescribed minimum for parcel registration. In states such as Mexico and Puebla with high population density, the average is 2.1 hectares. This can be compared with the average parcel size of private lands, which was 73.6 hectares in 1981. The size of parcels has had implications for household income generation. A 1960s study calculated that 84% of all *ejido* lands were insufficient to provide employment and adequate income for a peasant family--a basic definition of a minifundio. The limitations of parcel size, along with the unemployment problem that results from having only one child inherit the family parcel, have led to a high degree of reliance on off-farm work and outmigration.

This background helps explain some of the key provisions of the new law:

- **The constitutional obligation to redistribute land is removed**. (repealed sections X-XIV)

- **Land ownership limits have been maintained and clarified, and "improved" lands will not be reclassified for expropriation.** (title V; art. 117-121)

- **An Agrarian Attorney General (PA) will be presidentially appointed and land disputes will be settled by autonomous Agrarian Tribunals.** (title VII-X; art. 134-136)

- ***Ejidatarios* may sell, rent, sharecrop, or mortgage their lands as collateral for loans. They will no longer be required to work their land personally.** (chapt II, section VI, art. 78)

- ***Ejidatarios* may enter into joint ventures with outside investors, may form associations among themselves, and may sign long-term production contracts with outsiders.** (chapt II, section I, art. 46; title VI, art. 126, 127)

- **Legal restrictions on foreign investment are lifted, but a foreign equity capital limit of 49% remains.** (title VI, art. 130)

Although aiming to open up opportunities for investment in the agricultural sector, the law still retains limitations on size of holdings. The most significant is the establishment of a 2,500 hectare ceiling on the area of prime irrigated land that may be controlled by associations of peasants or private companies. This clause, as well as another which prevents individuals from owning stock in several agricultural companies, is offered as a safeguard against extreme land reconcentration.

For an *ejido* to dissolve itself and convert into private property the Agrarian Attorney General must approve the initiation of the process, upon solicitation of the *ejido* members. Two-thirds of the *ejidal* assembly, with at least three-fourths attendance, must vote in favor of dissolution. If this proportion of assembly members is not present at the first call, then only a simple majority needs to be present upon the second call. A representative from the Agrarian Attorney General as well as a notary public must be in attendance.

Criticisms of the new changes in agrarian law stem from fears of reconcentration of land and of the unequal bargaining power of *ejidatarios* in relation to the more powerful landowners and private investors. Critics say the safeguards against reconcentration found in the law are not as foolproof as they appear to be. In practice, specifications such as those for dissolution of an *ejido* are highly subject to abuse. There are historical precedents for significant pressure being placed by local *caciques* to call assemblies to achieve their own ends. It does not often happen in practice that an *ejidal* assembly would achieve the necessary 75% quorum to pass dissolution procedures on the first call, thus there is a possibility that some dissolutions may occur with as little as 33% of the total *ejido* represented on the second call.

In a 1991 survey taken before the law changed, two-thirds of ejidatarios interviewed indicated no willingness to sell their land. A "plurality" were in favor of production associations with private investors.

A final criticism of the changes in the agrarian reform law stems from the expectation of increasing social differentiation and inequality in the agricultural sector. This result is highly plausible. The flow of investment will be directed toward those *ejidal* operations that offer the best return. Estimates show that only about 10% of all *ejido*s have the necessary levels of organization, good quality land, and irrigation to be considered viable targets for outside investment. The regions of Mexico that are already highly commercialized and export oriented, such as the states of Coahuila, Sinaloa,

Sonora, and Guanajuato are best situated to benefit from the opening of the agricultural sector. By contrast states such as Jalisco, Michoacan, and Zacatecas where much of the production is in subsistence crops such as corn and beans, the level of opportunity may be much less. Already, most of the existing joint ventures are found in the more developed northern states of Sonora, Sinaloa, and Nuevo Leon.

During 1991, under previous relaxations, and in anticipation of the new law, there were 80 joint venture projects formed between ejidatarios and private firms. As of late 1992, just over 100 new projects had been created, but according to government sources, commercial banks are considering between 800 and 1000 joint venture credit requests. The hold-up in investment is blamed on lack of credit sources rather than the lack of initiative on the part of investors and ejidatarios.

Most investment is going into production agreements, in which private investors agree to purchase *ejidal* products, and agricultural processing operations. Examples: Nutrimex purchases soybeans, Grupo Visa purchases barley, and Gamesa purchases wheat; while BIMBO sets up cacao processing plants, and AGROINSA processes *ejidal* wheat into flour.

A recent study by the National Foreign Trade Bank of Mexico (BANCOMEXT) identified the problems hampering the creation of joint ventures as "poor budgeting, underestimation of operational and supply costs, *ejido* members' lack of experience with crops and new technologies, an ignorance of soil differences, high transportation costs, and an excessive product loss due to the distances between *ejid*os and processing plants." Additional problems included "attempts to transplant unfamiliar business practices, delayed responses to credit requests, unclear lines of responsibility, and scant follow-up to actions taken."

Many of the problems result from insufficient technical training and infrastructure. *Ejidatarios* may require additional technical assistance before they are viable investment partners. The physical infrastructure in the ejidal sector must be revitalized. The commercial banks, recognizing these shortcomings, are hesitant to lend.

The sluggishness of land sales is in great part due to the lack of accurate titling (or land record) information on the *ejidos*. Even though the government has promised an aggressive policy of land titling and the government has mandated a thorough survey, only 3,000 of the 28,000 *ejidos* presently have *ejidal* certificates, which must be converted into titles. Even before titles are handed out, the titling agency must first contend with an enormous backlog of land petitions that legally must be processed.

Estimates of these in-process petitions are as high as 32,000, involving over 3 million petitioners.

Previous attempts to modernize the agricultural sector through the expansion of irrigation infrastructure and the introduction of high-yield varieties resulted in regional polarization, with the irrigated districts of the north receiving the lion's share of benefits. The result has been a concentration of production, where almost 50% of agricultural production comes from 23% of total cropland and is produced by 19% of the rural work force. In addition to the concentration of production, there is also a concentration of land in the more modernized states. In Sonora, where 31% of the land is in the *ejidal* sector, the land Gini coefficient in 1970 was .79. Even the states with lesser agricultural modernization and higher percentages of *ejidal* lands, such as Jalisco and Chiapas, land Gini coefficients are .52 and .60. The current attempt at modernization may further exacerbate the problem if the unirrigated lands of the south are not seen as good investment possibilities by private investors.

The changes in agrarian law, if they are to benefit everyone, and not just those communities who are already well-integrated into the international market, must be complemented by other government investments in agriculture. Although there is a significant role for private investment--especially in rural industries--initial infrastructure development must be provided by government. Provision of information and legal and technical assistance, development of appropriate infrastructure, and supplying investment guarantees could help. If the changes in the agricultural sector are to truly achieve their promise of modernization, then the Mexican government must go further than simply opening the agricultural sector to investment. It must cultivate it as well.

This case study has drawn from: Backgrounder, No 914, The Heritage Foundation, Washington, DC.; Cornelius, Wayne A., "The Politics and Economics of Reforming the *Ejido* Sector in Mexico: An Overview and Research Agenda." LASA Forum, Vol XXIII, No. 3, (Fall 1992); Dresser, Denise. "Neopopulist Solutions to Neoliberal Problems: Mexico's National Solidarity Program." Current Issue Brief No. 3, Center for U.S. Mexican Studies, University of California, San Diego, 1991; *El Financiero International*, March 9, 1992; March 15, 1992; March 30, 1992; Heath, John Richard , "Evaluating the Impact of Mexico's Land Reform on Agricultural Productivity," World Development, Vol 20, No. 5, (May 1992) and Enhancing the Contribution of Land Reform to Mexican Agricultural Development, World Bank Working Paper #285, 1990; Ireson, W. Randall. "Landholding, Agricultural Modernization, and Income Concentration: A Mexican Example," Economic Development and Cultural Change, 1987; deJanvry, Alain and Sadoulet, Elisabeth. "Investment Strategies to Combat Rural Proverty: A Proposal for Latin America." World Development, Vol. 17, No. 8. (1989); Los Angeles Times, October 22, 1991, November 26, 1990; Villa-Issa, Manuel R. "Performance of Mexican Agriculture: The Effects of Economic and Agricultural Policies." American Journal of Agricultural Economics, Vol 72, No. 3, (August 1990)